CITY OF ART

kansas city's public art

By Tim Janicke

KANSAS CITY STAR BOOKS

CITY OF ART
kansas city's public art

WALKING MAN
(ON THE EDGE) (1995)

The Jonathan Borofsky figure appears to be striding across the roof of the Commons building at Johnson County Community College.

By Tim Janicke,
with additional material from
the staff of *The Kansas City Star*

Edited by Doug Worgul,
with additional editing by Tim Engle

Book design by Jeff Dodge

Published by Kansas City Star Books
1729 Grand Boulevard
Kansas City, Missouri, USA 64108

First edition

Library of Congress Control Number:
2001093175

ISBN 0-9709131-8-4

Printed in the United States of America
by Walsworth Publishing Company

To order copies of this book or prints
of the photographs, call StarInfo,
(816) 234-4636. For more information
about this and other fine books from
Kansas City Star Books, visit our
Web site at www.starinfo.com

SKY STATIONS (1994)

R. M. Fischer's creations top the pylons that support the south section of Bartle Hall, at Truman Road and Broadway in downtown Kansas City. Photograph by John Sleezer.

2 INTRODUCTION

16 CHAPTER 1
Tracing Our History

32 CHAPTER 2
Downtown

56 CHAPTER 3
Johnson County, Kansas

68 CHAPTER 4
Midtown

102 CHAPTER 5
Around Town

128 CHAPTER 6
The Art Museums

144 CHAPTER 7
The Legacy of
J.C. Nichols

156 CHAPTER 8
Country Club Plaza

180 AFTERWORD

182 LISTINGS AND MAPS

188 ACKNOWLEDGMENTS

CITY OF ART
kansas city's public art

By Tim Janicke

KANSAS CITY STAR BOOKS

◄

THREE WAY PIECE
NO.1: POINTS (1986)

The Henry Moore piece is part of the Kansas
City Sculpture Garden at the Nelson-Atkins
Museum of Art, Oak Street and Cleaver II
Boulevard.

INTRODUCTION
city of art

This is a tribute to a city of art: Kansas City. To its majesty, beauty, humor and power.

It is an appreciation of the city's art symbols, including the Bartle Hall "Sky Stations," the Nelson-Atkins Museum's "Shuttlecocks," "The Scout" in Penn Valley Park, the Power & Light Building and the J.C. Nichols Fountain.

This book is about Kansas City's most compelling art. We've left out the ordinary, the dingy and the disheveled.

To keep it simple, we concentrated on public art. Art you'll find outdoors. Art you don't have to pay to enjoy. We've organized chapters by geography in most cases, and sometimes by topic. And we've included maps so you can locate the artworks we've featured. The dates in parenthesis on each caption indicate the year the artwork was installed.

The real revelation in this book is how rich with public art our town has become. Consider what we've added to our art landscape in just 10 years:

"Shuttlecocks." "Sky Stations." "Bull Wall." "Triple Crown." "Light Steeple."

"Corps of Discovery." "Three Figures, Fifteen Elements" (shown at right). Then there's the Kemper Museum of Contemporary Art, Powell Gardens' "Island Garden" and the Community of Christ Temple in Independence. There are fountains, such as the new Henry Wollman Bloch Fountain north of the Liberty Memorial. And there's the Liberty Memorial itself, one of Kansas City's most enduring monuments, which got a $30 million facelift at the turn of the 21st century.

In this book you'll see traditional styles and modern; you'll see old art and new.

Mostly this is a picture book, the kind we hope you keep on your coffee table. We've tried to capture each sculpture or fountain looking its best. And we've tried to make each picture the kind of portrait you'd like to hang on the wall, above the sofa.

So enjoy this armchair tour of Kansas City's most alluring art. If you'd like to see it in person, this book's maps (see Page 184) will help you get there.

– Tim Janicke

►

THREE FIGURES,
FIFTEEN ELEMENTS (1996)

Joel Shapiro's sculpture sits in the median
between the inbound and outbound lanes of
the entrance road to Kansas City
International Airport. This is one of the three
distinct pieces that make up the sculpture.

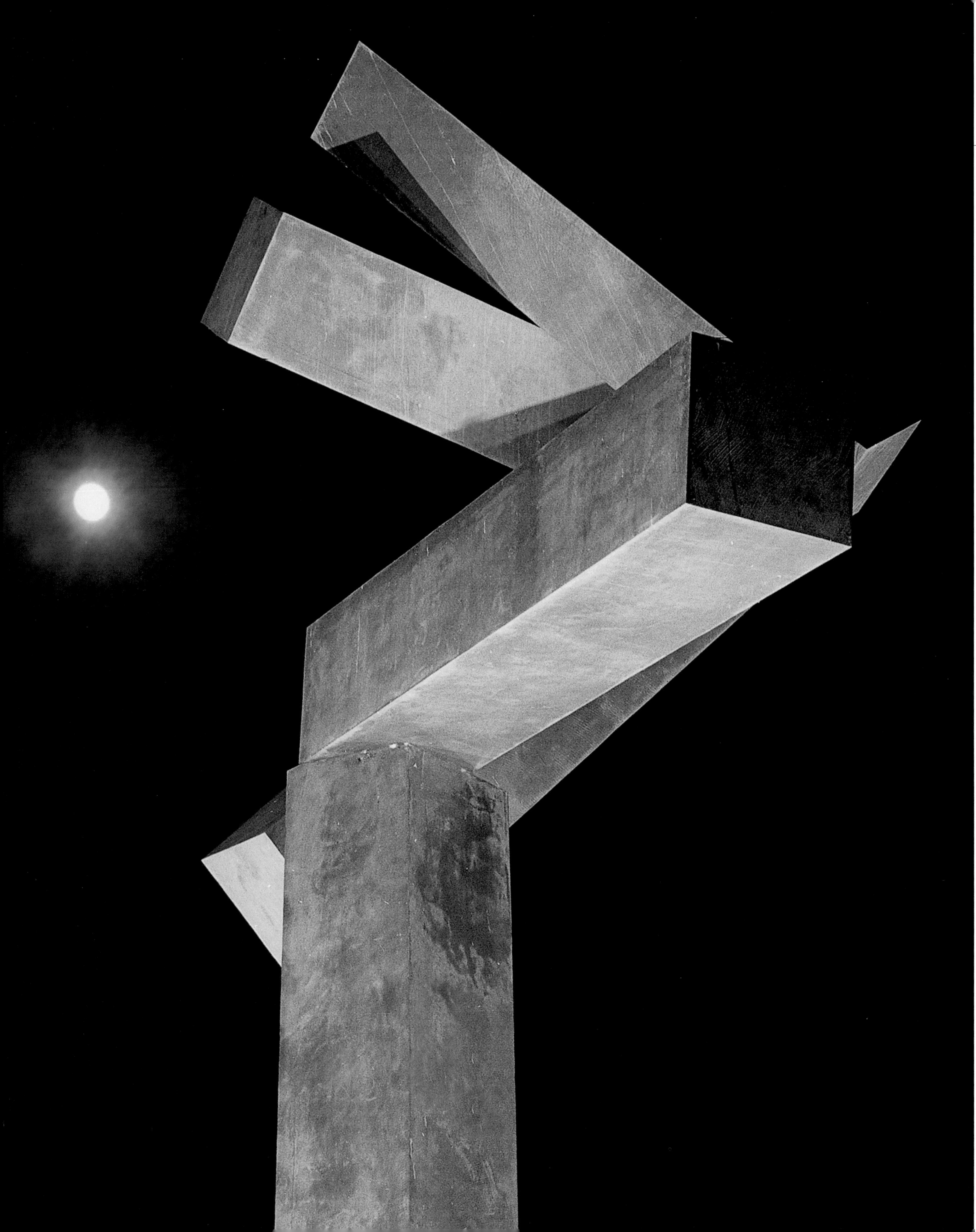

SPIDER (1997)

Louise Bourgeois' creature stands guard
on the front lawn of the Kemper Museum
of Contemporary Art, 4415 Warwick Blvd.

◄

BULL WALL (1992)

▲

BULL MOUNTAIN (1993)

Robert Morris' "Bull Wall," outside the
American Royal complex in the West
Bottoms, is two steel plates with
underground jets in between that force
steam through the cutouts. The steam
represents clouds of dust stirred by the
stampeding bulls. Morris used the
cut-out bulls to create "Bull Mountain,"
which is on a hill south of Interstate 670
and Genessee. "Bull Wall" photograph
by Keith Myers.

LIGHT STEEPLE (1994)

Architect Frank Lloyd Wright designed "Light Steeple" for Community Christian Church at 4601 Main St. However, because of budget limits and World War II blackouts, the steeple was not completed when the church was first built. Kansas City artist Dale Eldred and his wife, engineer Roberta Lord, undertook the project of completing the steeple in the early 1990s, but Eldred died before it could be achieved. Lord and members of the local arts community finished the project in 1994. The four 4,500-watt lamps shine on weekends and holy days and during the Christmas season. In this photo, streaks of rain are highlighted by the powerful lights.

THE ISLAND GARDEN (2001)

The Island Garden at Powell Gardens is
one of the area's newest pieces of public
art. The two-acre, three-tiered water
garden contains three cascading pools.
The water is pumped from a reservoir
underneath. Powell Gardens, a 915-
acre, not-for-profit botanical garden
about 35 miles southeast of Kansas City,
was established in 1988.

TRIPLE CROWN (1991)

This Kenneth Snelson sculpture
dominates a rolling green space south of
Crown Center at 2600 Grand Boulevard.
The dynamic aerial interplay of dozens of
glittering silver cylinders held in tension
by steel cables is intended to symbolize
the world's "multitude of contesting forces
pushing and pulling at one another." The
faux bovines were part of Kansas City's
CowParade exhibit in the summer of 2001.

HENRY WOLLMAN
BLOCH FOUNTAIN (2001)

Kansas City's newest – and priciest –
fountain, featuring 232 water jets, was
installed in the median of Pershing Road
west of Main Street. Though the Bloch
Fountain is owned by the city's parks
department, it is operated by Union
Station. The fountain is on from 6 a.m. to
midnight during warm-weather months.
Five-minute "high shows" are scheduled
on the hour and half-hour.

TRACING OUR HISTORY

city of art

Detail from the Alexander Phimister
Proctor's "Pioneer Mother" sculpture.

CHAPTER 1: TRACING OUR HISTORY
city of art

You can trace the history of Kansas City by looking at its sculpture.

The statues in Penn Valley Park reflect the city's origins. "The Scout" represents the American Indian population before white settlement. On the far west side of the park, "Scout" sits on his horse, shading his eyes as he gazes northward across the city's skyline. East, across Broadway, white settlers are represented by "Pioneer Mother" (shown at left), which depicts a weary woman holding a child as she rides a horse sidesaddle across the prairie. Two men walk beside her, one on each side.

Meriwether Lewis and William Clark were among the first white men to arrive in what became Kansas City. A statue in Case Park commemorates the explorers. The 18-foot-tall bronze, "Corps of Discovery," shows Lewis and Clark, their interpreter Sacagawea, and Clark's slave, York, as they gaze over the confluence of the Missouri and Kansas rivers. A plaque nearby reads:
On September 15, 1806 Meriwether Lewis and William Clark returning from the Pacific stood on this point and recorded in their journal that this was a "commanding situation for a fort and that from the top of the hill you have a perfect command of the river..."

Just to the south of the Lewis and Clark monument is a statue of James Pendergast, representing the political machine that controlled the city for several decades. Pendergast was an alderman from the West Bottoms in the late 1800s. His brother Tom Pendergast, Kansas City's longtime political boss, had the statue erected with public funds after his brother died.

"The Muse of the Missouri" symbolizes the significance of the Missouri River. Situated in a downtown median between Eighth and Ninth streets on Main, this bronze nude holds a net from which fish are spilling.

A huge bust of jazz saxophone player Charlie Parker celebrates Kansas City's jazz age of the 1920s and '30s. The statue, in a pocket park at 17th Terrace and Vine Street, faces east, toward Parker's former haunts at 18th and Vine.

"Pioneers," a statue in the median of Broadway at Westport Road, commemorates the establishment of Westport as a stop on the Santa Fe, California and Oregon trails. It shows John C. McCoy, who platted the town of Westport in 1833; Alexander Majors, a Westport businessman and partner in the Pony Express; and Jim Bridger, a frontiersman who operated a dance hall and saloon in Westport.

PIONEER MOTHER (1927)

The Alexander Phimister Proctor sculpture – which weighs 16,000 pounds – sits on a ridge just west of the Liberty Memorial in Penn Valley Park. "Pioneer Mother" depicts weary pioneers traveling westward across the plains. Howard Vanderslice, an early member of the Kansas City Art Commission, sponsored the memorial in remembrance of all pioneer mothers, and to honor his parents, who migrated from Kentucky to Kansas after he was born.

CORPS OF DISCOVERY (2000)

"Corps of Discovery," a representation of
Lewis and Clark by Eugene Daub,
overlooks the confluence of the Missouri
and Kansas rivers from Case Park at
Eighth and Jefferson streets. Standing
18 feet tall, the sculpture depicts
Meriwether Lewis, William Clark and
Sacagawea, their Shoshone guide and
interpreter. Not shown here are York,
Clark's slave, and Seaman, their dog.

MUSE OF
THE MISSOURI (1963)

The 30-foot-tall "Muse of the Missouri," by Wheeler Williams, occupies a median on Main Street between Eighth and Ninth streets. It honors Lt. David Woods Kemper, who was killed in action in Italy during World War II. The monument was commissioned by his father, James M. Kemper Sr., and presented to the city. "Muse of the Missouri" depicts the Greek goddess of song, poetry, and arts and sciences.

THE SCOUT (1922)

Dedicated in 1922 as a memorial to local
Indian tribes, "The Scout," by Cyrus E.
Dallin, depicts a Sioux scout on horseback.
It was originally cast for the Panama-
Pacific Exposition in San Francisco in 1915.
After the exposition, "The Scout" was tem-
porarily exhibited in Kansas City. Kansas
Citians became so enamored of it that they
raised $15,000 to buy it. The sculpture is on
a hillside in Penn Valley Park east of
Southwest Trafficway. Over the years "The
Scout" has become something of a civic
mascot. The image has been used in
endeavors as diverse as art exhibitions
and bank advertising campaigns. Kansas
City sent a half-scale replica of "The Scout"
to sister city Seville, Spain, for display at
the 1992 World's Fair. The work was subse-
quently presented to Seville as a gift.

JAMES PENDERGAST (1913)

Pendergast was a First Ward alderman and the older brother of Tom Pendergast, who ran Kansas City's political machine in the early 20th century. The younger Pendergast had this statue, by Frederick C. Hibbard, erected with tax money. The memorial was dedicated in 1913 in Mulkey Square downtown and later moved to Case Park at Eighth and Jefferson streets.

BIRD LIVES (1999)

This Robert Graham sculpture sits in
a pocket park at 17th Terrace and Vine,
looking toward 18th and Vine, one of
saxophonist Charlie "Bird" Parker's
early hangouts.

PIONEERS (1987)

"Pioneers" honors (from left) John C. McCoy, founder of Westport; Alexander Majors, a Westport businessman and partner in the Pony Express; and Jim Bridger, a frontiersman who operated a dance hall and saloon in Westport. The piece, by Thomas Beard, is on the east side of Broadway north of Westport Road.

Detail from "Muse of the Missouri"
by Wheeler Williams

DOWNTOWN
city of

CHAPTER 2:
DOWNTOWN
city of art

Downtown Kansas City hosts an eclectic collection of our town's public art. People often think of the whimsical "Sky Stations" sculptures atop Bartle Hall and the art-deco Power & Light Building when they think of downtown art. But downtown is rich in other sculpture, architecture and fountains as well.

Many of the ornate downtown buildings with significant architectural details were constructed in the first half of the 20th century. Intricate carvings, gargoyles and other design flourishes adorn these structures. The Cathedral of the Immaculate Conception, with its landmark gold dome, got a makeover at the millennium.

And there's modern art, such as the "Rain Thicket" fountain, and the "Modern Communication" sculpture outside the city's emergency communications center.

Jackson County political boss Tom Pendergast left a legacy to public art in Kansas City. through his political operative, presiding judge Harry Truman, sold the public on a 10-year capital improvements project that included a new art-deco city hall. The building opened in 1937, and the plaza and its fountains bowed the following year.

CITY HALL SEA HORSES (1938)
"Lug" by Paul Jennawein

Now in front of Kansas City police headquarters at 12th and Locust streets, this piece by Robert Merrill Gage was originally dedicated in 1921 at 15th Street and the Paseo. In 1949 it was moved to 59th Street and the Paseo. It was installed in its present location in 1973. The monument honors police killed in the line of duty.

Two rows of four fountains, each 10 by 20 feet wide, line the sidewalks leading to the south entrance. The northernmost fountain on each side displays a spraying seahorse and two spraying dolphins. Three smaller fountains follow the grade to 12th Street, each slightly lower than the one behind it. A dolphin emerging from a seashell sprays into the smaller pools.

The public nicknamed the two seahorses "Cut" and "Lug," in a sarcastic nod to Pendergast. "Cut" referred to the payroll deduction that patronage employees were forced to contribute to the Pendergast machine; "Lug" stood for the payroll lug – an additional deduction – sent to the political machine to finance election campaigns.

Noted sculptor Paul Jennawein designed the fountains and the sculpture. Critics described his neo-classical style as a merging of art nouveau with antiquity. Though the public apparently loved the plaza area, several design problems plagued the project: The fountains leaked into the underground parking garage and the sidewalks flaked. The fountains were turned off for eight years, until 1970, when the city finally spent $125,000 to fix the problems.

That hasn't been the only dry period for the fountains. During World War II, city officials decided to turn the pumps off to save the $1.50 a day it cost in

electricity to run them.

In the 1950s, children swimming in the fountains vexed city officials. On July 10, 1956, *The Kansas City Star* photographed an 8-year-old boy, one Larry Severance, taking a dip in a City Hall fountain as city health inspector John Irwin took a water sample. *The Star* reported on July 11 that the sample was clean and that the city had decided to leave the swimmers alone, "though no invitations are being issued by the city" to swim.

Over the years, people have moved farther away from downtown, and children no longer flock to City Hall to cool off. Now Cut, Lug, the dolphins and their pools are back to doing what they were built to do – look impressive.

▲

The Transamerica building at 12th and Main streets frames a decorative Kansas City street lamp.

CATHEDRAL OF THE
IMMACULATE CONCEPTION (1883)

The Cathedral of the Immaculate Conception at 411 W. 10th Street originally had a
copper dome. The spire was covered with gold leaf during a renovation in 1960.
During another renovation in 2000-01, fresh gold leaf was added to the dome, which
had begun to show wear and tarnish. In addition, stonework and bricks were cleaned
and repaired, deteriorating ornamental metal repaired, and exposed wood painted.
Constructed in 1883, the cathedral is the mother church of the Catholic Diocese of
Kansas City-St. Joseph and considered the primary church of the bishop.

SUNDIAL

At the northeast corner of
Ninth Street and Broadway

ART IN THE DETAILS
OF KANSAS CITY BUILDINGS

In Kansas City, Kansas, a fireman gargoyle decorates the roof of a former fire station at 2 S. 14th Street.

This metal inlay decorates the art-deco Hotel Phillips at 12th and Baltimore streets. The 20-story, 217-room architectural masterpiece, restored at a cost of $20 million in 2001, first opened in 1931.

Municipal Auditorium, on 13th Street between Wyandotte and Central, was built in 1934 in the art-deco style and has intricate carvings on its face.

▲

The face of a lion peeks out from an apartment building in the Quality Hill neighborhood downtown.

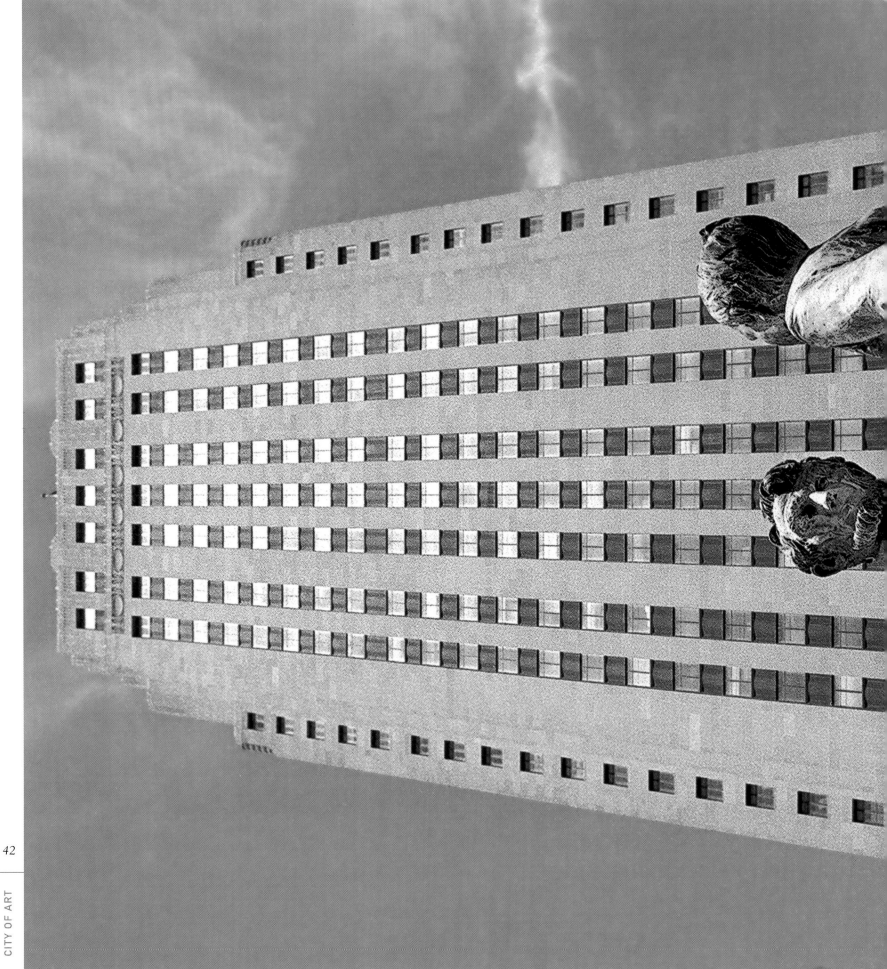

ABRAHAM LINCOLN

ABRAHAM LINCOLN AND HIS SON TAD (1986)

This 2,500-pound, 10-foot tall statue of Abraham Lincoln and his son, Tad, by Lorenzo Ghiglieri, is outside City Hall on 12th Street between Oak and Locust streets. The $150,000 statue was commissioned by Kansas Citian Orville Anderson, an insurance salesman, photographer and Honest Abe fan.

▲

HARVESTER (1987)

This piece by Nancy Graves is the focal point of the UMB courtyard
at the bank's headquarters at 11th and Walnut streets. The sculpture
depicts corn, wheat, a windmill, a tractor part and a rake.

▶

RAIN THICKET (1981)

The fountain by William Severson and
Sanders Schultz is in the Oppenstein
Memorial Park at 12th and Walnut streets.

RODINRODANNADANNA (2000)

This Donald Lipski sculpture adorns the exterior
wall of the Poindexter Garage at Ninth and
Central streets. The $200,000 piece features a
30-foot diameter ring of 18 fiberglass reproduc-
tions of the world-famous sculpture "The
Thinker" by Auguste Rodin. In daylight the
74-inch-high figures look as if they are made of
bronze; at night they glow translucent blue, from
a system of interior lights. The artwork's name,
of course, is a nod to the character made
famous by Gilda Radner on "Saturday Night
Live." Lipski's perspective on the 19th-century
masterwork was commissioned by two Kansas
City businesses: DST, a record-keeping firm for
the mutual funds industry, and CDFM2
Architecture. An internationally exhibited artist,
Lipski is known for making sculptures utilizing
familiar objects.

POWER & *light*

Photographs by David Pulliam

Power & light

She's gorgeous, with a look that's all her own. She's slender, statuesque and accessorized. She absolutely glows – in three colors, no less. And people are crazy about her. Always have been.

The Power & Light Building is downtown Kansas City's most distinctive skyscraper and one of the country's best examples of art-deco design.

Not long ago, the office building at 14th Street and Baltimore Avenue was only about one-third occupied. Then along came a massive downtown Kansas City redevelopment plan – named for the building – that promised new life for the venerable structure. But it went nowhere.

Early in the new century, the architecture firm BNIM took over three-plus floors, including the refurbished two-story foyer. As a result the Power & Light Building found itself nearly 70 percent occupied. But in the autumn of 2001 the skyscraper's major tenant, moviehouse chain AMC Entertainment Inc., announced it would be moving out.

The specialness of the building isn't lost on its tenants.

"I think it's one of the more significant points of reference in Kansas City, a point of reference like the Liberty Memorial or Union Station," says architect Ted Seligson, whose firm (these days known as Foss Seligson & Lafferty) has been in the Power & Light Building since 1970. "It's a handsome building. It

Powerful floodlights installed in the setbacks illuminate the 34-story Power & Light Building.

was done at a time when a lot of quality was utilized in building.

"Also, it's very accommodating for offices. It has a great view. Even on the lower floors, it's quite an urban experience you get."

Construction on the Kansas City Power & Light Co.'s sky-high home took, remarkably, only 19 months. The building, designed by the local architecture firm of Hoit, Price & Barnes, was completed in late 1931.

The Power & Light boasted an opulent first-floor lobby connected by a grand marble staircase to the second floor. The first floor had a two-toned Italian Travertine marble floor and wainscoting and columns of Florido Cream and Blue Belge marble. Most interior walls of the building were finished in American walnut. Corridors featured patterned terrazzo floors and Tennessee marble wainscots and plaster cornices.

Sunburst motifs decorate the panels above the first-floor display windows.

The street-level display windows on the Baltimore and 14th Street sides once featured electricity-using appliances. Today, BNIM Architects uses the windows to spotlight some of the firm's building projects.

Ornament, as architects call it, is everywhere. A recurring theme is energy, especially the sun. This was, remember, the Power & Light Building. Architect Seligson says the style of art deco employed in Power & Light's design is based on American Indian art.

The lit-up lantern at night

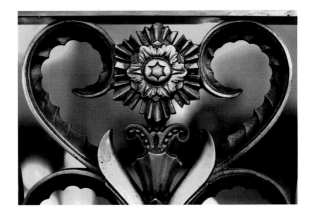

Floral designs define the second-floor balcony railings.

Lightning bolts and birds on power lines appear on metal doors in the first-floor lobby.

Huge 500- and 1,000-watt incandescent bulbs illuminate the four beveled glass windows near the top of the building.

"Indians used the sunbursts and sun themes, and those, combined with the theme of electricity in this case, worked beautifully."

There's a dramatic sunburst above the former main entrance on the Baltimore side. Sunburst motifs also appear above the first-floor display windows and on fourth-floor balconies.

If you're a fan of architectural froufrou, the best examples are in BNIM's space in the former foyer. Geometric patterns including floral motifs and, yes, sunbursts, shine on columns, beams, friezes, staircase balustrades and radiator grills. Out in the elevator lobby, sunbursts brighten up the floor and the elevator doors. There are plenty of other examples throughout the building, including way up high. What's that crowning the stone face of the lantern at the top of the building? Yep, more sunbursts.

Once darkness descends over downtown, it's hard to miss the Power & Light Building. The night-light show produced by the building is as distinctive as the architecture. The very top of the dome glows a solid red. But the lights below – red, green, amber and white – were designed to complete a rotation every 30 seconds.

"These many shades will not be apparent all at once," *The Kansas City Star* reported in August 1931. "Rather, they will flicker and blend one into the other, appearing successively. It will be as though a diamond of grotesquely immense proportions were being turned slowly this way and that in sunlight so that it would glitter and sparkle, giving off light beams of seemingly unending variance of color."

The effect originates from banks of colored floodlights that shine up from the 31st floor setback into the lantern and from more colored lights inside. Four prismatic glass windows, each 26-1/2 feet tall and 6-1/2 feet wide, contribute to the magic. Between 1974 and 1982, the changing of the lights was halted because KCP&L couldn't find parts for the rotating mechanism.

In 1991 KCP&L announced it would be moving employees out of its namesake skyscraper and into a shiny new office building at 1201 Walnut. But even now, customers – about one a day – still turn up at the Power & Light Building to pay their electric bills.

– *Tim Engle,*
Kansas City Star reporter

POWER & LIGHT by the numbers
▶ Height: 476 feet 6 inches, according to architects in 1931.
▶ Cost: About $4 million in 1930-31.
▶ Floors: 32 or 34, depending on what one considers a floor. The 30th floor is the highest occupiable floor.
▶ Elevators: Eight passenger elevators, a freight elevator and an elevator that runs between the 29th floor and the bottom of the lantern (32).

◄   ▲

A BRUSH OF TIME, 1994

Alexander Austin's mural covers the
north side of the building at 3217 Troost
Ave. The work depicts the struggle of
African-Americans at the time Martin
Luther King Jr. was leading civil rights
marches.

Colorful murals embellish
retaining walls on the west
end of Avenida Cesar E.
Chavez, near Kemper Arena
and the American Royal
complex.

ONE PERCENT *for art*

Public art in Kansas City, Missouri, typically comes from one of two sources.

The first is the city's one-percent-for-art program, which sets aside one percent of the cost of public construction projects for art.

This program commissioned, among others, "Bull Wall" by Robert Morris at the American Royal complex, "Sky Stations" by R.M. Fischer atop Bartle Hall, and "Modern Communication," the Terry Allen sculpture shown here, which is adjacent to Kansas City's emergency communications center on Locust, north of the police department.

The one-percent program, administered by Kansas City's Municipal Art Commission, employs a panel of experts, project principals and community representatives to select artists and their works. Final approval of a project is by the City Council.

The second source for public art is private individuals and groups. "Corps of Discovery," a larger-than-life-sized bronze by Eugene Daub of famed explorers Meriwether Lewis and William Clark, their interpreter Sacagawea and Clark's slave, York, falls into this category. The City of Fountains Foundation and the William T. Kemper Foundation commissioned this public monument. It overlooks the confluence of the Missouri and Kansas rivers in Case Park. Sculptures such as this also usually go before the commission for approval.

Friction sometimes develops when individuals and groups circumvent the arts commission. Although city law says that public art must go through the commission, it's a law that's sometimes flouted.

Art installed outside Kansas City, Missouri, doesn't fall under the jurisdiction of the arts commission. Artworks at Johnson County Community College, for instance, come under the auspices of the college's art gallery director.

MODERN COMMUNICATION (1994)

This bronze depicts a windblown executive standing on his briefcase with his fingers in his ears and his tie fluttering across his face. The sculpture, by Terry Allen, is outside Kansas City's emergency communications center next to police headquarters. Allen said in 1994 that he tried to explore how people communicate and how institutions communicate – "...whether it's what we are subjected to in terms of the outside bureaucracies that we deal with, or our own bureaucracies that are in our own selves, which I think can be every bit as frustrating, every bit as hilarious," he said.

JOHNSON COUNTY

city of art

TEAM ILLUSION (1992)

The David Hickman sculpture is
seen here reflected in a pond at
Sar-Ko-Par Trails Park at 87th
Street Parkway and Lackman
Road in Lenexa.

TWO ON BEAM (1997)

The Magdalena Abakanowicz
piece is installed in an interior
courtyard at Johnson County
Community College.

CHAPTER 3: JOHNSON COUNTY
city of art

Johnson County, Kansas, has sometimes been criticized for lacking the culture of its urban neighbor Kansas City, Missouri. Perhaps some of the criticism is justified, but there are significant artworks to be found in the county, especially at Johnson County Community College.

The director of the college's gallery, Bruce Hartman, has built a collection of cutting-edge contemporary art. He presides over an interior gallery as well as what's become a sculpture park on the college's campus.

Several significant pieces dominate the campus, beginning with "Flight of Imagination," a kinetic polished-steel sculpture that twirls in the wind. Installed in 1983, it was one of the first pieces in the college's collection.

In 1995 artist Jonathan Borofsky oversaw the installation of his 6-foot-tall "Walking Man" sculpture on the roof of the Commons Building. First-time viewers of the sculpture, unsure if the figure is real, are often unsettled by what appears to be a man striding purposefully along the edge of the Commons roof (see photograph at the front of this book).

"Walking Man" is one of five pieces in the Oppenheimer-Stein Sculpture Collection at the college. The collection focuses on contemporary works by nationally and internationally recognized sculptors and features diverse styles. Judith Shea's seated female figure "Between Thought and Feeling" is part of the collection, as is Magdalena Abakanowicz's "Two on Beam" (shown at left).

Elsewhere in Johnson County, public art ranges from the contemporary to the whimsical to the traditional. In Leawood, "Growing," a stainless-steel sculpture by Richard Hunt, rises 21 feet above the grounds of City Hall.

In Sar-Ko-Par Trails Park in Lenexa, six red, white and blue bicycles fly high over the pond in "Team Illusion," a sculpture by David Hickman of Dallas. The "Children of the Trails Memorial," by Kwan Wu, honors children who made the trek west on the Santa Fe, Oregon and California trails. Fashioned from bronze and stainless steel, the 14-foot sculpture rises above a reflecting pool between the Johnson County Courthouse and the county administration building in Olathe.

BETWEEN THOUGHT AND FEELING (1988)

Both pieces shown here are on display in an interior courtyard at Johnson County Community College. The bronze and cast stone sculpture above is by Judith Shea. Grant Kenner's steel sculpture, right, rotates in the wind.

FLIGHT OF IMAGINATION (1983)

HARE AND BELL (1988)

The Barry Flanagan piece depicts a leaping animal, gracefully and unexpectedly poised atop a massive bronze bell. It's outside the Johnson County Community College library in an interior courtyard.

▲

PERFORMANCE PIECE (2000)

Dennis Oppenheim's gigantic fiberglass
and steel knotted chimney is embedded
with trumpets. It was loaned to Johnson
County Community College in 2000 and
then permanently acquired by the college
in 2001.

▶

WOMAN WITH
PACKAGES (1996)

This Louise Bourgeois piece, a bronze
with a dark patina, is in an interior
courtyard on the JCCC campus.
Bourgeois has said the piece may
represent herself and her feelings
about her role as a wife and mother.
She said the "packages" pinned to the
figure could symbolize shopping or
children.

◄

CHILDREN OF THE
TRAILS MEMORIAL (2000)

Olathe artist Kwan Wu's work depicts a young pioneer boy and girl
running through 14-foot-tall stainless steel arches that symbolize
a rainbow. The arches reflect sunlight from different angles
throughout the day onto the bronze children. The sculpture and its
reflecting pool are between the Johnson County Courthouse and
the county administration building in Olathe.

▲

GROWING (2001)

This sculpture can be found on the grounds of Leawood City Hall.
Artist Richard Hunt said the theme of the piece is growth. "I had
the idea of wanting to make something upward-moving – growing,
something to reflect Leawood's own growth." He said the
sculpture was sanded with upward-moving strokes, lending it a
texture that makes it feel as if it's trying to pull upward.

MIDTOWN
city of art

JOY OF LIFE (2001)

This piece, by Robert MacDonald, is on the grounds of the Stowers Institute for Medical Research.

CITIZEN SOLDIER (2001)

"Citizen Soldier" (2001), by Jim
Brothers, depicts a Vietnam-era
soldier and the same man 30 years
later as a member of the Veterans
of Foreign Wars. The statue, at the
VFW national headquarters at 34th
and Broadway, is one of several by
the Lawrence sculptor that depict
soldiers. Brothers' work is included
at National D-Day Memorial at
Bedford, Virginia.

CHAPTER 3: MIDTOWN
city of art

Some of Kansas City's most vener-
ated public art is located in the
midtown area, between downtown and
the Country Club Plaza. Here you'll
find modern sculpture such as
Alexander Calder's "Shiva" and Kenneth
Snelson's "Triple Crown," both on the
Crown Center campus. But traditional
pieces also stand out, such as "St.
Martin of Tours," the sculpture that is
the centerpiece of the Volker Memorial
Fountain, as well as the statue of Jacob
L. Loose at the east entrance to Loose
Park. Kansas City's biggest monument,
the Liberty Memorial, occupies the
high ground of midtown.

A computer controls the 232 water
jets in the new Henry Wollman Bloch
Fountain on Pershing Road between the
Liberty Memorial and Union Station.
With special lights illuminating each jet,
the Bloch fountain is the most dramatic
Kansas City fountain.

Traditional sculptures make up some
of the oldest public art in the midtown
area. "The Scout" was installed in Penn
Valley Park in 1922; "George
Washington" was installed in
Washington Square Park, north of the
Westin Crown Center hotel, on Nov.

11, 1926, the day the Liberty Memorial
was dedicated. A year later to the day,
"Pioneer Mother" was dedicated in
Penn Valley Park, west of the memorial.
"Pioneer Mother" and "The Scout"
appear in the Tracing Our History section of this book.

Hallmark, the Kansas City greeting
card company, and its owners, the Hall
family, are responsible for some of the
newer works of public art in midtown.
In 1973, the Halls opened Crown
Center, a hotel, shopping, entertainment and office complex situated
between Union Station and Hallmark's
headquarters. The complex displaced
blight: Signboard Hill, an ugly billboard-
and weed-covered hill at Main Street
and Pershing Road. The Halls installed
several pieces of art, notably "Shiva" and
"Triple Crown."

It made sense for the city to fix up
Union Station and the Liberty
Memorial after the Halls cleaned up the
neighborhood. With the recent installation of the Bloch fountain and the
renovations of Union Station and the
Liberty Memorial, the area has become
more of a magnet for both Kansas
Citians and tourists.

A computerized pump room controls and choreographs a ballet of water spouting from 232 water jets. Distinct pops of air mean that the jets are shooting their long-range missiles of water — sometimes as high as 60 feet. A sheen of water an eighth of an inch thick reflects Union Station and the Liberty Memorial on the 102- by 146-foot oval black granite face. At night each water jet becomes an illuminated light saber.

Kansas City's newest work of art – a fountain – may in fact be its most dramatic. Dedicated to H&R Block founder Henry Bloch, the Henry Wollman Bloch Fountain opened in fall 2001 in the median of Pershing Road, just west of Main Street. The fountain's designer, Claire Kahn Tuttle, said she intended something that was fresh, yet formal.

"It was important to create a work with a kind of dignity that hopefully would last for many years and would feel right in that space," says Tuttle, of Los Angeles-based WET Design. "It's a modern form, it's not a derivative form. But it has a simplicity and purity about it."

WET Design also created the dancing waters at the Bellagio Hotel in Las Vegas and a fountain at Disney's Epcot in Florida. BNIM Architects and J.E. Dunn Construction Co. of Kansas City completed the project. The H&R Block Foundation commissioned the fountain as a retirement gift for Bloch, who stepped down in 2000.

"We definitely weren't going to give him a gift only he would enjoy," says Morton Sosland, a director of the foundation. "No gold pen, no watches for Henry." Bloch and his brother Richard founded H&R Block, the largest tax and financial services provider in the country.

Foundation officials wouldn't say how much the new fountain cost. But Kansas City Parks and Recreation Director Terry Dopson says it is easily the city's most expensive fountain. For example, the smaller, less-complex Firefighters Fountain in Penn Valley Park cost $1.5 million.

With the new fountain comes a $500,000 endowment to cover maintenance costs.

The fountain will operate from 6 a.m. to midnight during warm months. Five-minute "high shows" are scheduled on the hour and half-hour.

— Matt Campbell,
Kansas City Star reporter

Looking west through the Henry Wollman
Bloch Fountain, which opened in 2001

The jets of the Bloch Fountain can shoot as high as 60 feet in the air. The fountain sits in a median on Pershing Road, between Union Station on the north and the Liberty Memorial (pictured) on the south.

THE GEORGE
WASHINGTON MEMORIAL (1926)

This statue, by Henry Mervin Shrady, sits in
Washington Square Park, northwest of Pershing
Road and Grand Boulevard. It's a replica of the
original in New York City. The sculpture stands 16
feet high and rests on a pink Minnesota granite
base. Contributions from 109,000 citizens provided
the funds to pay for it.

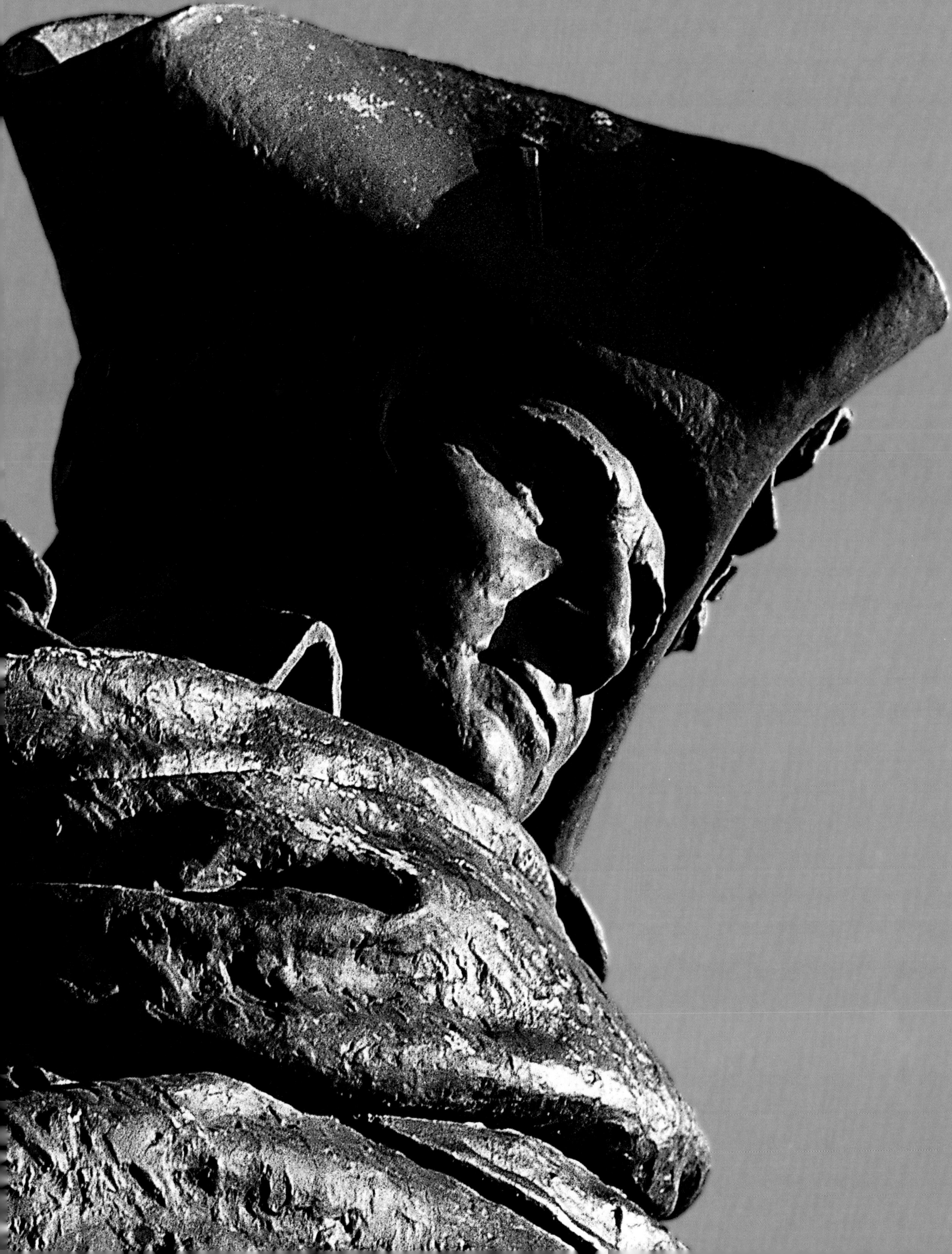

◄

SHIVA (1974)

This steel sculpture, by Alexander Calder, is on the southwest corner of Pershing Road and Grand Boulevard, on the Crown Center campus. It represents the Hindu mythological god of destruction and reproduction.

▼

The stone lions in front of the Kansas City Life Insurance Co., Broadway and Armour Boulevard, accent the classical motifs of the building's beaux-arts design.

LIKE PETALS UNFOLDING (1987)

These bronze statues of children by Dennis Smith cavort in front of the headquarters building of American Century Investments at 45th and Main Streets.

THE STOWERS *institute*

When Jim and Virginia Stowers decided to use their personal fortune to establish the Stowers Institute for Medical Research, they also decided to make the buildings and grounds a place of beauty.

Jim Stowers founded Twentieth Century Investors in 1958. Forty years later, the mutual funds company, now called American Century, had assets of more than $70 billion. The Stowerses, both cancer survivors, provided almost all the $1.6 billion endowment that finances the institute.

The institute is in the former Menorah Medical Center at Rockhill Road and Volker Boulevard. The old hospital was expanded and now has 600,000 square feet of offices. Outside, the 10 acres the four buildings sit on were beautified, too. "Hope for Life" (shown at right) is a 32-foot-tall, 16,000-pound stainless-steel sculpture that represents the double helix of a DNA molecule. It stands at the entrance to the institute.

A landscaped park leads from the entrance around the west side of the institute to the back. A series of lime-stone-edged cascading pools meanders across the grounds, eventually leading to the sculpture "Joy of Life," by Carmel, California, artist Robert MacDonald. Kim and Nate Harbur of Overland Park donated the sculpture to

honor organ donors. Their son Luke was a liver transplant recipient.

A parking lot off 50th Street, just east of Rockhill Road, is available to the public. A pavilion near the highest point of the campus gives folks a place to view the grounds as well as the Kansas City skyline.

Geometric patterns of plants complement the park and the adjacent building. Plants include gingko, willow, Kentucky coffeetree, witchhazel, potentialla, purple coneflower, yarrow and thyme.

The back side of the institute, facing Volker Boulevard, is a wall fountain. Cascades of water fall from the upper stories of the building down the face of the north side to pools on the street level.

▲

JOY OF LIFE (2000)

The Robert MacDonald sculpture is the centerpiece of a fountain at the Stowers Institute.

▶

HOPE FOR LIFE (2000)

This Larry Young piece was made in Kansas City by the A. Zahner Co. The fabricators used a 22-inch solid bronze model to map a three-dimensional image. They then cut stainless steel to size to match the model and joined the pieces together.

VOLKER FOUNTAIN (1958)

Volker Fountain is the centerpiece of the park officially known as Frank A. Theis Memorial Mall. The apartments in the background here are on Oak Street.

By the time William Volker died in 1947, he'd become the leading philanthropist in Kansas City. He'd helped finance Research Hospital, the Helping Hand Institute, the city's first welfare department, a legal aid bureau and the University of Kansas City, now UMKC. And he'd served on the school board, personally establishing a pension fund for teachers by donating $100,000. He funded plenty of other causes, about $10 million worth, *The Kansas City Star* reported.

The businessman had quietly amassed and distributed a fortune in Kansas City. He made money first by making and selling picture frames and then by diversifying into sales of other household goods, such as window shades and linoleum. But he was as delighted to give his money away as he was to earn it.

He did it all quietly. At most public events, he was the guy hanging back, standing in the shadows. So people surmised that he would have tried to avoid the honor of having a fountain named after him.

In late 1947 Kansas City Mayor William E. Kemp appointed a committee to raise funds and decide how to honor him.

A 1958 *Star* column explained: "He was clearly motivated by the simple wish to throw a little lightness in a life of darkness and distress. This might take the form of an undreamed-of graduation dress for a girl of a poverty-stricken family. And he once remarked, 'It never hurts to spoil old people; old ladies ought to have money to jingle in their pockets.'"

By 1950 the committee and the city had decided to honor Volker by building the Volker Memorial Fountain south of the Nelson-Atkins Museum of Art.

The selection committee picked well-known Swedish sculptor Carl Milles to create the statuary. *The Star*'s editor, Henry J. Haskell, was chairman of the fountain committee. He gushed that "Milles was generally regarded as the most distinguished living sculptor."

Milles decided to sculpt St. Martin of Tours, a 4th century Roman soldier who removed his cloak on a bitter day in 332 A.D., cut it in two with his sword and gave it to a beggar. According to legend, Christ appeared to Martin in a vision that night, saying, "What you have done for that poor man, you have done for me." After the vision, Martin devoted his life to Christ.

In Milles' sculptural interpretation, St. Martin rides a horse. Beneath him is a figure of the beggar, hand outstretched, waiting to receive a piece of the cloak. On the right, a centaur and an angel sit below St. Martin watching. On the left side, an angel playing a flute looks down at St. Martin from his perch on a staff. Milles liked to add a touch of humor to his sculptures; he put a watch on the wrist of the seated angel.

It ended up taking more than 10 years from the time the fountain was planned until its unveiling in 1958. Milles worked slower than expected. First he planned to deliver the statuary in 1953, then '54, finally delivering it in

1955, right before he died. And the city had problems clearing the land. The land south of Brush Creek Boulevard, now called Cleaver II Boulevard, and east of Oak had been designated for a cultural mall with a large rectangular lake. In anticipation of these changes, Brush Creek had been diverted through a culvert underneath the land.

Designers placed the fountain in the middle of the park. The statuary occupied a long, irregularly shaped pool, with two fountain jets placed on each side in smaller pools. From Volker

Boulevard, on the south, people could look past the Volker Fountain to the Nelson Gallery in the background.

The parks board dedicated the Volker Memorial Fountain and Volker Park on Sept. 20, 1958. Shortly thereafter, board chairman Frank Theis noticed that the upper angel was listing. Park staff rescued it and eventually remounted it on a stronger staff.

The open spaces around the fountain attracted a diversity of patrons: families, romantic teen-agers and Art Institute sketchers. In the 1960s the park

The seated angel wears a wrist watch.

The waterfall behind the Volker Fountain is 272 feet long.

▲

The view across Theis Memorial
Mall has the Nelson-Atkins
Museum of Art in the background.

became a hangout for hippies and other counterculture types. There were war protests, rallies and rock concerts. People also began gathering in the fountains on hot days to beat the heat. In 1966, the park board renamed the park Frank A. Theis Memorial Mall to honor Theis' contributions to Kansas City parks.

The Volker Memorial Fountain was removed in 1993 so Brush Creek could be redirected from its culvert under the park back into the open, for flood control as well as for beautification. The

fountain was reinstalled in 1996, this time adjacent to Volker Boulevard on the south.

When the Volker Fountain was reinstalled, the parks department also added to it, installing a cascading waterfall behind it. Visible only from the north side of Brush Creek, the new waterfall is 272 feet long. Water cascades from a wall behind the fountain down twin sets of steps in Brush Creek. The waterfall serves as a backdrop for a natural amphitheater constructed on the north banks of Brush Creek.

◄

Jeanette Klein of Kansas City sculpted these figures of a man and a woman for the wall fountain in Loose Park, unveiling them in 1942. The bowls originally filled with water and then spilled into a basin. The flowing water was eliminated in 1946.

▼

This statue of Jacob Loose, by Rudolph Evans, stands in Loose Park at 51st Street and Wornall Road, just south of the Country Club Plaza. Loose's wife, Ella, gave the land for the park to the city in 1927 and donated the statue of Loose in 1941.

LIBERTY *memorial*

90

CITY OF ART

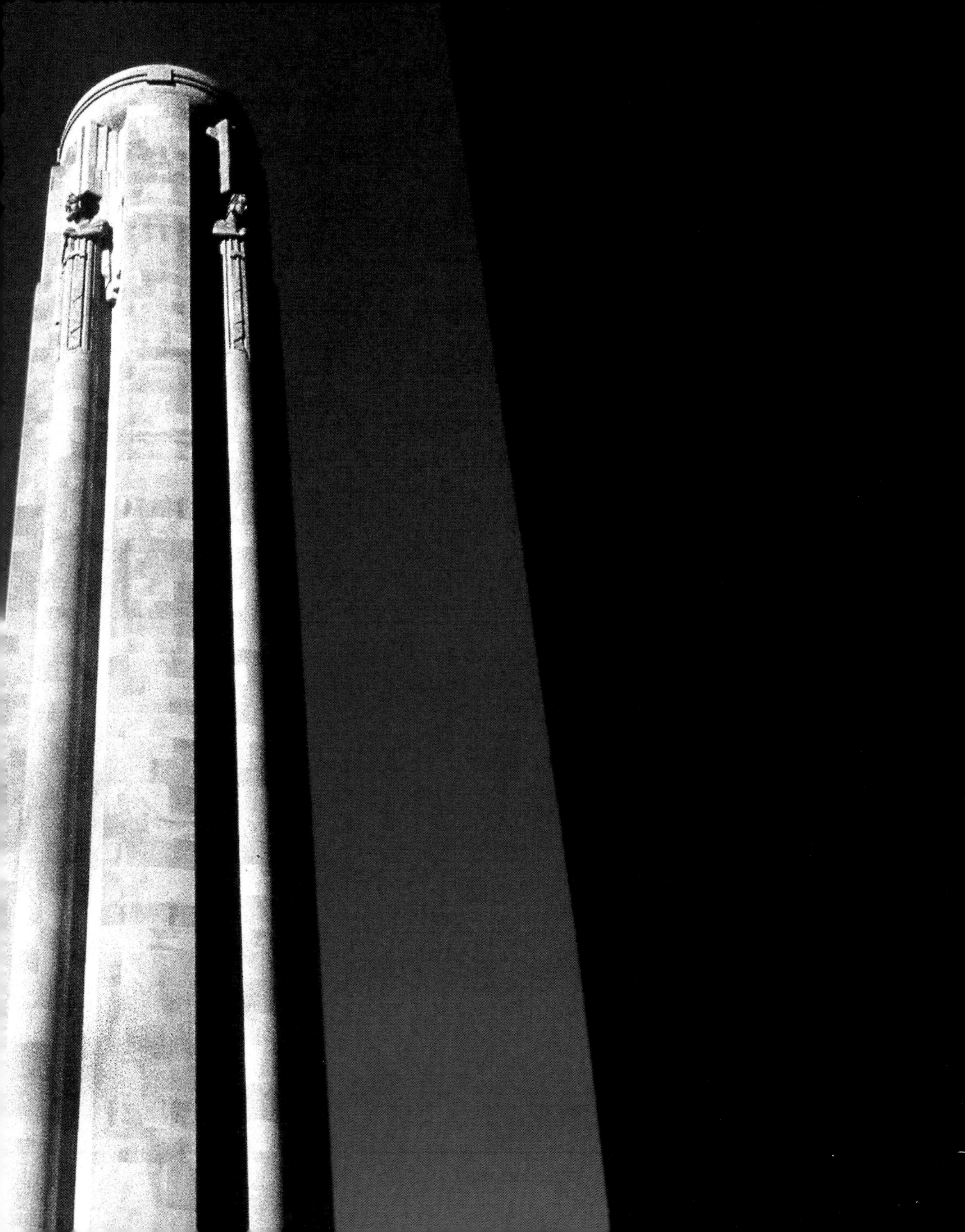

Kansas City's most obvious example of public art is the Liberty Memorial.

The memorial's shaft rises 217 feet from its base. Four 40-foot-high sculptures of guardian spirits – symbolizing courage, honor, patriotism and sacrifice – stand guard over the metropolitan area from atop the monument. At night a red glow, representing an eternal flame, illuminates the pinnacle of the tower.

Conceived in 1918, in the days immediately after World War I, the Liberty Memorial represents Kansas City's effort to honor those who fought and died in the war. A 10-day fund-raising campaign in 1919 generated more than $2.5 million for the memorial. The site, south of Union Station, in Penn Valley Park, was dedicated in 1921 before world politicians, military leaders, the American Legion national convention and more than 100,000 Kansas Citians. President Calvin Coolidge dedicated the finished monument on Armistice Day, Nov. 11, 1926, before a similarly sized crowd.

At the turn of the 21st century, the city began renovating the memorial. This renovation was scheduled to be finished in 2002. The city had closed the monument when engineers discovered the foundation had deteriorated; they were afraid the memorial might collapse. In 1998 Kansas Citians approved a sales tax to raise $30 million to renovate the monument and provide $14.7 million for

maintenance.

The renovation angered a small but vocal group opposed to some aspects of the project. The group contended that too much of the original memorial design had been altered. Work was slowed while preservation groups were consulted about the design. Eventually the city decided to ignore the protesters and proceed with its original plans.

The renovation means that hundreds of World War I artifacts in storage can go on display. The memorial always had a small museum, but improvements will mean much more space. The renovated memorial will have a new museum entrance on the south side. Besides the shaft and the museum, the memorial includes two buildings, containing artworks and the names of Kansas City soldiers who died in the war, two sphinxes, a frieze and two fountains.

The sphinxes represent memory and the future. The frieze, depicting the sufferings of war and the blessings of peace, is 148 feet long and adorns the north wall, facing Union Station. The two fountains, also part of the renovation, lie below and in front of the frieze.

Sculptures representing four guardian spirits are near the top of the monument.

◄

Busts of the victorious Allied leaders of World War I line the wall that faces Pershing Road.

TOM *corbin*

You can smell the sculptor's wax melting in a blue Rival Crock-Pot in the corner. Opera plays on the boom box over on a workbench across the basement. Under a fluorescent shop light, Tom Corbin dabs clay on a sculpture. Corbin makes bronze tables, benches, lamps, chandeliers, sconces and sculptures in his River Market studio. He may be the most prolific artist in Kansas City – and chances are, you've never heard of him.

But you've probably seen his work: the figures at the Firefighters Memorial Fountain in Penn Valley Park, the Children's Fountain in the Northland and Kauffman Memorial Gardens near the Country Club Plaza, for example. And the life-size figures of Ewing and Muriel Kauffman outside Kauffman Stadium.

You won't find Tom Corbin lingering over a latte at the coffee shop with the Kansas City culture crowd, bemoaning offenses against art. He's up about 6 a.m. reading the newspaper, drinking coffee and running, biking or swimming. A triathlete, he's usually training to compete. At 5 feet 11 and 180 pounds, he's trim.

"I don't quite fit into the traditional artistic crowd," Corbin says. "Early in my career I was intimidated by people with credentials. But over time I realized those credentials don't necessarily indicate the amount of talent an individual has or their dedication to succeed at their craft."

Though he's moved toward a more personal, expressive style in recent

THE CHILDREN'S FOUNTAIN (1995)

This Corbin playground scene is on North Oak
Trafficway in Waterworks Park.

▼ A statue in Kauffman
Memorial Gardens

years, Corbin's public sculpture is mostly traditional. His sculpture of firefighters looks just like, well, firefighters. His bronze children are snapshots of a playground scene.

After graduating from college with a business degree in 1976, he landed a job in Kansas City selling corrugated boxes. He stuck with it for two years and then quit.

"I had my fill of that," he says. "I felt I had to get into something more creative."

Corbin switched to an advertising career and began to learn about sculpting and bronze casting. He hit up Miller Nichols for work.

"I asked him if he needed any original art on the Plaza," Corbin says, smiling at his own naivete. Nichols said no, but he did need some repairs made. Corbin fixed assorted cherubs and other pieces. That led to his first commission, two bronze plaques at the original Nichols headquarters and four bronze benches that still sit around the fountain on the northeast corner of Ward Parkway and Wornall Road. The Plaza work led to a commission to do an eagle for a war memorial in Richmond, Missouri.

Corbin quit the ad business in 1986 to be a sculptor full time. His technical ability to produce lifelike statuary helped get him commissions. He sculpted the Kauffmans from photographs; he says he used himself as a model for the Firefighters Fountain, dressing in a bunker coat and helmet and studying himself in the mirror.

He hasn't done as many public art commissions in recent years, concentrating instead on his burgeoning business in home furnishings — lamps, tables and the like. But when he does produce a public piece, the price tag is usually in six figures.

▲ Clay busts from the creation of the Children's Fountain sit on a shelf in Corbin's basement studio.

▲ The artist still likes to draw. Here he produces an illustration for a Corbin Bronze product guide.

◄ One of Corbin's early commissions was to produce bronze benches on the Plaza.

◄

Over the years Corbin's sculpture style has evolved from very representational works to a more elongated, stylized human form.

▲

Corbin says that of the statues at the Firefighters Fountain, he most prefers the figure of the fireman that stands behind the fountain.

Tom Corbin's World

Tom Corbin's public art is on display around the city. Look for these examples:

▶ Kansas City Firefighters Memorial Fountain, Penn Valley Park

▶ The Children's Fountain, Waterworks Park on North Oak Trafficway

▶ Kauffman Memorial Gardens, 4800 Rockhill Road

▶ Ewing and Muriel Kauffman statues, southwest side of Kauffman Stadium

▶ United Nations Peace Memorial Statue, Community of Christ (formerly RLDS) headquarters in Independence

▶ Wyandotte County Korean/Vietnam War Memorial, Wyandotte County Lake

▶ The Rev. John Williams Statue, the Paseo and Truman Road

▶ Plaza benches, Ward Parkway and Wornall Road

Kauffman Memorial Gardens (1995)

The gardens at 4800 Rockhill Road include four Corbin works among the fountains.

THE KANSAS CITY
FIREFIGHTERS MEMORIAL (1991)

This fountain, at Penn Valley Park, was Corbin's
first big public art commission.

AROUND TOWN
city of art

THE SALVATORE GRISAFE MEMORIAL (1968)

This memorial, sculpted by Jac T. Bowen of Kansas City, stands in the median of the Paseo at 16th Street. The 18-foot monument memorializes Salvatore Grisafe, who was killed while thwarting the robbery of two women in 1964. It represents the out-stretched arms of a young person, striving for greater goals.

city of art

Past Powell Gardens' elegant entrance and down a winding path sits one of Kansas City's newest and classiest pieces of public art: the Island Garden at Powell Gardens.

Through a canopy of trees, the path widens to a pier that reaches out over a 12-acre lake. From the pier, visitors can *ooh* and *ahh* at the new two-acre, three-tiered water garden. The 15-foot top pool cascades into the 45-foot middle pool, which in turn cascades into the 75-foot lower pool, which appears to cascade into the lake below – but that's an illusion. A transparent Lexan shield guides the water back to a reservoir and pumping system.

Powell Gardens, a 915-acre, not-for-profit botanical garden about 35 miles southeast of Kansas City, opened in 1988. Set among rolling hills, the park features gardens, lakes, ponds, trails and meadows. The Visitor Education Center has an indoor conservatory, terrace gardens, a garden store and a cafe. A chapel with a dramatic view of the gardens is often the scene of weddings.

The Powell Gardens staff spent two years constructing the new Island Garden. Individuals, trusts and foundations donated the $1.6 million to finance it. Whisper-quiet, the elaborate new pumping system recirculates 95,440 gallons of water underneath the existing Powell Gardens lake.

More than 800 plants, including 84 water plants, decorate the new garden.

Powell Gardens and the Island Garden are open year-round. Heated water in the Island Garden circulates until the first hard freeze. A variety of plants spring from containers that sit just below the water line, including daffodils, tulips and lilies.

Powell officials say the 600-foot-long stone wall that surrounds the Island Garden is the "longest living wall garden." More than 250 plant varieties grow from the wall, including plants originating in the rocky soil of Missouri's Ozarks, as well as plants from around the world. Visitors walk on stone-lined paths and sit on wooden benches.

Powell Gardens is open daily from 9 a.m. to 6 p.m. April through October, and 9 a.m. to 5 p.m. November through March. Take U.S. 50 east from Kansas City; the access road to the gardens is on the north side of the highway and is well-marked to both eastbound and westbound traffic. Call (816) 697-2600 for information about admission prices and special events.

POWELL *gardens*

Potted seasonal plants sit right below the surface of the Island Garden at Powell Gardens. Heated water circulates until the first hard freeze.

SPIRIT OF FREEDOM (1981)

The Richard Hunt sculpture provides the focal point for the fountain on the south-west corner of Cleveland and Brush Creek Boulevard.

◄

COMMUNITY OF CHRIST TEMPLE

The Temple was dedicated in 1992. On the corner of River Road and Walnut in Independence, the dramatic 300-foot roof resembles a corkscrew or seashell that twists into a spire. The church was formerly known as the Reorganized Church of Jesus Christ of Latter-Day Saints.

▼

UNTITLED (1996)

This is a detail of the 15-foot sculpture by Garth Edwards outside the fire station at 6600 Truman Road that features representations of firefighters and flames in a three-tiered design that includes a small building.

THE RACE IS NOT
ALWAYS TO THE SWIFT! (1999)

This Ken Ferguson piece sits at the entrance to
Lakeside Nature Center in Swope Park.

This carved sphinx is one of two that flank the
entrance to the Scottish Rite Temple at Linwood
Boulevard and the Paseo.

Urban palisade (1994)

You'll find this in front of the Central Patrol offices of the Kansas City Police Department at 1200 East Linwood Blvd. The work was commissioned as part of Kansas City's One Percent for Art program.

THE CONCOURSE

The dramatic concourse at St. John Avenue and Gladstone Boulevard was constructed as part of the original Kansas City parks and boulevards system. Steps descending from the back of the colonnade lead into the woods adjacent to Cliff Drive.

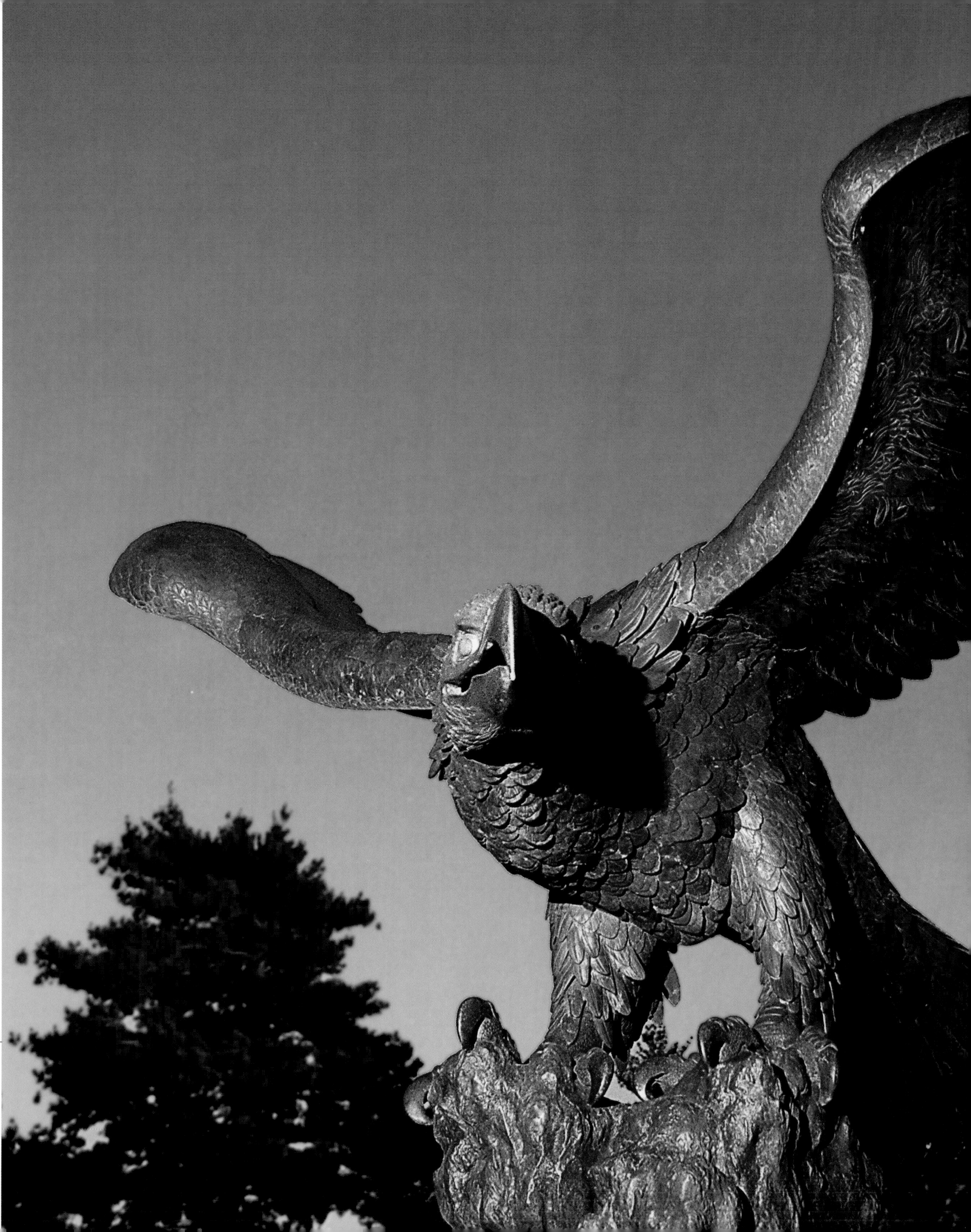

THE EAGLE (1935)

Created by an unknown Japanese sculptor, "The Eagle" stood for years in the courtyard of a temple in Japan. The J.C. Nichols Co. presented the sculpture to Kansas City after purchasing it from an art dealer in New York. It's now displayed in the median of Ward Parkway at 67th Street.

▲

▶

AVENUE OF THE TREES

Kansas City architect Edward B. Delk designed the Avenue of the
Trees, south of Meyer Circle, as a memorial to the 440 Kansas City
men and one woman who died in World War I. The stone eagle is one
of two that top the pilasters of the entranceway.

BRUCE R. WATKINS DRIVE

Bridges over Bruce R. Watkins Drive were redesigned for beauty.
Cantilevered sidewalks were added to make both sides accessible to
neighborhoods. Decorative lamps adorn many of the support pillars
along the freeway, which opened in October 2001.

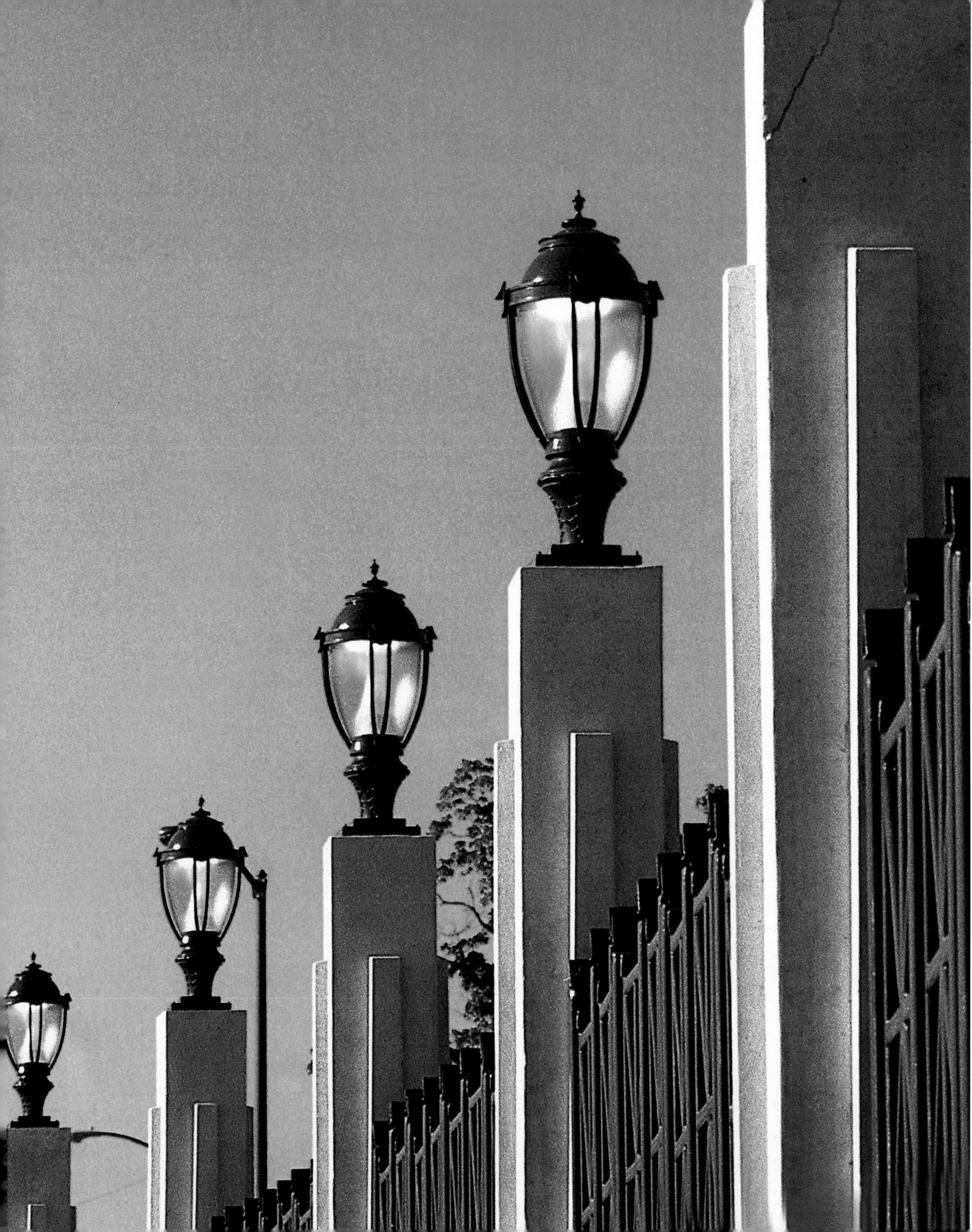

The J.C. Nichols Co. placed works
of art in its residential developments,
such as this collection of columns on
Ward Parkway at Gregory Boulevard.

ELDEN *tefft*

Most current artists who cast in bronze probably owe a debt of gratitude to Elden Tefft. After completing bachelor's and master's degrees in fine art at the University of Kansas in 1951, Tefft made it his mission to reinvent bronze-casting techniques.

As a professor of art at KU, he endorsed casting to an art community that thought sculpture was valid only if it was hand-carved. Tefft saw it as a lost art that needed finding. It was a place where he thought he could make his mark in the art world.

"I'd been thinking about bronze casting," Tefft says, "about casting using the lost-wax process, but the process was almost lost." Tefft says that only the art guilds in Europe were using the process when he began to advocate its resurrection in the 1950s.

Although there were other casting techniques for art, such as sand casting,

none could capture the complicated detail and form that the lost-wax process did. Other methods just weren't applicable to art, Tefft says. Though the lost-wax process sounds mysterious, it's really a method to reproduce a piece of sculpture or a model by using a rubber-like material as a mold.

The rubber is applied to the sculpture, allowed to cure, then it's pulled away from the sculpture and coated with wax. This rubber mold is filled with plaster and silica. Then the rubber is removed, revealing a wax image of the original sculpture. The wax image is then immersed in plaster and silica. Once the plaster hardens, it is placed in a furnace and heated to 1,000 degrees. The wax inside melts and vaporizes. Tefft still uses the process at the southeastern Lawrence studio he shares with his son, Kim.

On a night when they are casting, the blast of the gas furnace sounds just like a jet engine. Tefft, son Kim and other artist-volunteers wear face masks, long mint-green fireproof coats and heat-resistant spats as they sidestep across the studio floor with a crucible of molten bronze. They move deliberately – at 2,000 degrees, the 100-plus pounds of shiny, yellow metal is hot enough to incinerate a hand or a foot. The men tip the crucible and a bright stream of liquefied bronze streams into a plaster and silica mold. Once the bronze has cooled, the plaster cradle is chiseled away, revealing the bronze art.

In the 1950s Tefft evangelized about the lost-wax process to other artists, and

▲

Dressed in protective mask and fire-proof coat, Elden Tefft supervises a bronze pour at his Lawrence studio.

◄

Workers carry the molten bronze in a crucible.

►

It took 15 years for Tefft to finish his masterpiece, this 10-foot-tall sculpture of Moses that sits in front of Smith Hall at the University of Kansas.

by 1960 he was conducting international conferences in the technique. A KU convocation of 100 international artists, led by Tefft in 1960, evolved into the International Sculpture Center. Tefft was its first director. Now based in Hamilton, New Jersey, the group boasts 5,000 members.

On his way to teaching others the technique, Tefft has left a legacy of art, especially around the KU campus and Lawrence: a bronze Jayhawk in front of Strong Hall, a bronze bust of William Allen White inside the KU journalism school, a bronze lion at Lawrence High School, just to name a few.

But his most highly regarded piece sits across from the Kansas Union in front of Smith Hall, the center for religious studies. It took 15 years and six separate castings to finish the 10-foot, filigreed-bronze sculpture of Moses.

Tefft retired from KU in 1990; he says he "graduated." But he still works full days either in the studio or perhaps in Burcham Park down by the Kansas River, where he pounds a chisel into a limestone sculpture called "Keeper of Our Universe."

Elden Tefft (foreground) directs the casting of a bronze sculpture. The masks, coats and spats protect the workers from the 2,000-degree molten bronze.

▶

Kim Tefft examines the bronze torso that had just been cast.

THE ART MUSEUMS
city of art

SHUTTLECOCKS (1994)

"Shuttlecocks" by Claes Oldenburg and
Coosje van Bruggen, is the whimsical set
of badminton birdies that litter the
grounds of the Nelson-Atkins Museum of
Art. (Photograph courtesy of The Nelson-
Atkins Museum of Art.)

KANSAS CITY *sculpture park*

SEATED WOMAN (1986)

"Seated Woman" is a Moore sculpture that is part of the collection donated by the Hall Family Foundation

Art lovers can take walking tours of outdoor sculpture at three Kansas City art institutions. The best by far is the Nelson-Atkins Museum of Art's Kansas City Sculpture Park, but there are also significant pieces nearby on the grounds of the Kansas City Art Institute and at the Kemper Museum of Contemporary Art.

From dawn to sunset, dog walkers, art lovers and troops of grade-schoolers meander among the masterworks at the Sculpture Park. The park is between Oak Street and Rockhill Road and along Cleaver II Boulevard. It's open seven days a week during daylight hours. A renovation of the museum and the grounds will be completed in 2006. Until then some sculpture normally on display will be in storage.

"A sculpture garden of precisely the right sort" is how *New York Times* art critic John Russell described the park when it opened in 1989 as the Henry Moore Sculpture Garden.

The collection of monumental out-door works has grown considerably from the initial 12 bronzes by Moore to more than 30 pieces by leading American and international artists. A high point was the addition of the much-debated "Shuttlecocks" by Claes Oldenburg and Coosje van Bruggen in 1994.

"I think it's turned out to be a much greater success than anybody could have imagined – in size, quality and, most importantly, the difference it's made in the relationship between the museum and the community," museum director Marc Wilson says.

"It's also been the critical mass in terms of attracting visitors nationally and internationally."

The Hall Family Foundation has been a major supporter of the Nelson's sculpture collection from its inception. In 1986 the foundation made a long-term loan to the museum of 56 works by British artist Henry Moore, including 10 of his monumental bronze sculptures that were installed outdoors; later those works were given to the museum permanently.

LARGE INTERIOR FORM (1986) by Henry Moore

The foundation has continued to add pieces, including the recent acquisition of five major sculptures by Isamu Noguchi, one of which, "Ends," is part of the sculpture park.

"Shuttlecocks," the four gigantic fiberglass-and-aluminum badminton birdies, each weighing 5,500 pounds, were a gift to the museum from the Sosland family. Although initially controversial in Kansas City, the "Shuttlecocks" attracted national and international neknown when they were installed in 1994.

There's more than just sculpture in the park, though. In a new book celebrating the 10th anniversary of the sculpture park, Deborah Emont Scott, the museum's chief curator and curator of modern and contemporary art, inventories some of the plantings that were part of that original design: "more than 50,000 daffodils; more than 10,000 Japanese yew; 100 American linden, gingko, crab apple, Norway spruce and river birch trees; and more than 4,000 square feet of Baltic ivy."

The E.F. Pierson Sculpture Garden, a smaller collection near the main Nelson building, contains mostly figural works by 19th- and 20th-century masters including Auguste Rodin, Pierre-Auguste Renoir and Gaston LaChaise.

A new permanent addition commissioned specifically for the sculpture park is Judith Shea's "Storage." Shea's series of figural components "evolve" from clothed female torso forms to a man's overcoat and finally into a fully realized female figure in a sheath-style dress; they were installed in 1999 in the East Garden against the poetically stained limestone wall of Pierson

SHEEP PIECE (1976)

Henry Moore was commissioned
to produce "Sheep Piece," a second
casting of a monumental four-ton
sculpture that he had created for
his estate in England. It was the
first piece installed on the grounds
of what became the Kansas City
Sculpture Park.

Garden, where a large locust tree casts dappled shadows.

The most ambitious addition is an installation of 30 figures, each slightly different from the other, by Polish-born artist Magdalena Abakanowicz. Cast in bronze from models made of plaster-soaked burlap, they are headless and backless – shells of humanity evocative of war victims or prisoners.

The museum's sculpture initiative, a plan to establish the Nelson as a major center for modern sculpture, was an outgrowth of the Moore acquisitions.

As a result, the museum now owns the largest collection of monumental Moore bronzes outside of England and the third-largest collection of Noguchi sculptures in the country.

Marc Wilson, as he looks to the future, says it is crucial that the artworks never overwhelm the landscape.

"One of the beauties of this is that you do feel that you're in a natural place, and we want to protect that feeling," he says. "It's what distinguishes us from so many others, where you lose the sense of nature because it's overpowered by an excessive proliferation of sculpture."

STANDING FIGURES (1999)

Magdalena Abakanowicz's sculpture includes 30 headless, standing bodies. It has been removed from the Kansas City Sculpture Garden during expansion at the Nelson-Atkins Museum of Art but will return in 2006 when construction is completed. (Photograph courtesy of The Nelson-Atkins Museum of Art.)

Next door to the Nelson, at 44th and Warwick Boulevard, is the 18-acre campus of the Kansas City Art Institute, founded in 1885 to teach visual arts and design. The most significant outdoor artwork at the art institute is "East Gate Piece" by the late Dale Eldred, a monumental metal and wood sculpture just inside the east gate to the school. There's also a nearly life-size sculpture of famed Kansas City painter Thomas Hart Benton nearby.

Across Warwick from the Art Institute is the Kemper Museum, which opened in 1994. Although the most significant pieces of art are inside, it's worth a visit to inspect the spider sculpture outside. In 1997 the Kemper acquired two Louise Bourgeois spider sculptures and put them on permanent display outdoors. A small one crawls up the wall at the Kemper's front doors; the larger one, weighing 1,600 pounds and measuring 11 feet high and 20 feet in diameter, is installed nearby on the front lawn.

◀   ▲

THE THINKER (1951)

Left: "The Thinker" (1951), by Auguste Rodin, was a gift to Kansas City by Grant and Mathilde Rosenzweig. The sculpture has been removed from the north entrance to the Nelson during construction but will return sometime in 2006, when expansion is finished. (Photograph courtesy of The Nelson-Atkins Museum of Art.)

THREE BOWLS (1999)

"Three Bowls" by Ursula von Rydingsvard, sculpted from cedar and graphite. (Photograph courtesy of The Nelson-Atkins Museum of Art.)

◄   ▲

STORAGE (1999)   RUSH HOUR (1995)

Judith Shea's "Storage" was commissioned for the   The George Segal sculpture,
Kansas City Sculpture Park. Shea told the Nelson: as well as "Storage" have
"They lean propped up against the wall essentially as been removed from the sculp-
if forgotten or stored. The truncated clothing forms   ture park, but will return when
provided an essence – no extremities, no movement;   construction is finished in
it was a way to express the essence of human pres-   2006. (Photograph courtesy of
ence." (Photograph courtesy of The Nelson-Atkins   The Nelson-Atkins Museum
Museum of Art.)   of Art.)

EAST GATE PIECE (1966)

Artist Dale Eldred contributed this
piece to the Kansas City Art Institute.
It's just inside the east gate of the art
school, off Oak Street across from
the Nelson-Atkins Museum.

▲

This lifelike statue of Thomas Hart Benton is found on the campus of the Kansas City Art Institute. Benton, known for his paintings and murals, was once a teacher at the school.

▶

SEVEN VIEWS OF
THE GRAND CANYON (1995)

This Dale Eldred piece is a steel sculpture in seven parts on the west lawn of the Kemper Museum of Contemporary Art.

J.C. Nichols installed the classic Meyer Circle Fountain in 1925 at the south end of his trendiest suburban development, the mansions of Ward Parkway.

The fountain sits in the center of a traffic circle situated between the north- and southbound traffic lanes of Ward Parkway, the western terminus of Meyer Boulevard and two other side streets. As a result, the view most Kansas Citians get of this fountain is from a car, rather than from a contemplative stroll through a park.

The circle and Meyer Boulevard were named for August R. Meyer, the first president of the Kansas City parks board and one of the people credited with the pushing for parks and boulevards here.

Much of the Meyer Circle statuary had been on display in Venice for more than 300 years before the Nichols company bought it and moved it to Kansas City for the fountain. Sculptors carved the figures from Cararra marble.

Over time the fountain has become as famous for the vehicles circumnavigating it as for the fountain and its marble artworks. Drivers played NASCAR around the traffic circle for years, usually emerging from the other side of the circle unscathed, sometimes wrecking. One traffic survey found that 37 percent of the accidents involved sideswiping; 25 percent were collisions

with other cars; and of the remaining reasons for vehicular mayhem, 12 percent were cars that left the roadway. Some of the accidents produced fatalities.

In 1978 a homeowner on the southwest corner of the circle reported that he'd rebuilt the stone wall adjacent to the intersection "eight to 10 times." By 1979 it was reported in *The Kansas City Star* that there were, on average, 40 accidents a year at the circle, making it one of the most dangerous intersections in the city. The Kansas City parks board then announced it was going to leave the fountain alone but straighten Ward Parkway and prohibit access to the side streets.

The public protested. People were in love with the circle and the fountain in the middle of it. The Committee to Save Meyer Circle organized and convinced the parks board and the city to stop messing with the landmark, danger or not. Eventually, changes in traffic signals and a gentle straightening of the roadway alleviated the traffic problems.

In the 1980s the citizenry objected to renovations to the fountain. The wall of the fountain was rebuilt, but people complained that it was too high. Eventually the parks board gave in to pressure and had the wall sawed off so that passing motorists could better see the pool inside.

The original fountain sprayed water

The statuary and spraying equipment for the Meyer Circle Fountain have been replaced several times since the fountain's installation in 1925.

from 16 nozzles. Like many of the early Kansas City fountains, the Meyer Circle Fountain was built only to squirt – the spray went down the drain. It was occasionally turned off during water shortages and finally replumbed in the '60s with a recirculating pump after the city starting charging the parks board for water – one month in 1965, the bill was $1,100.05. Subsequent remodeling has added nozzles and water pressure, making the display more dramatic.

The Meyer Circle Fountain is the centerpiece of the fountains adorning Ward Parkway. The other pedestals and reflecting pools are elegant, but none has caught the imagination or engendered the love of the public like the dramatic sprays of Meyer Circle.

MEYER CIRCLE
FOUNTAIN (1925)

The Meyer Circle Fountain is the most magnificent of the fountains along ritzy Ward Parkway.

BELINDER COURT
FOUNTAIN (1925-27)

This Mission Hills fountain mirrors
the design of the Meyer Circle
Fountain on Ward Parkway, supplying
the centerpiece for a traffic circle.

J.C. Nichols imported statuary from Europe to complete
the landscaping of his residential developments in com-
munities such as Mission Hills.

VERONA COLUMNS
and other j.c. nichols pieces

Winding roads pass majestic mansions in the affluent community of Mission Hills, Kansas. At the bottom of a hill, at the intersection of three streets, are the Verona Columns. The columns and its fountain are there because early 20th-century Kansas City developer J.C. Nichols found and bought a number of art pieces, often in Europe, to furnish his housing developments.

The Verona Columns and the statuary at Meyer Circle are some of the finer pieces that the Nichols company acquired during shopping trips to Europe. Most of the pieces wouldn't qualify as great art, but Nichols' housing developments had no art and he thought they needed some kind of ornamentation, so the pieces seemed to fit in.

In a 1924 speech, Nichols told a group of developers: "I don't believe there is anything we have done that is adding more to the individual character and creating a more distinct environment than the placing of these ornaments."

The Nichols company sometimes commissioned new pieces of art, but it was also adept at recycling. For instance, the company bought the Country Club Plaza's 8,000-pound Neptune statue, cast from lead, for its scrap-metal price. And the children of J.C. Nichols bought the statuary for the J.C. Nichols Fountain from a Long Island estate.

According to the files of *The Kansas City Star,* Nichols spotted the Verona Columns while on a trip to Verona, Italy, in 1922. In 1927 his company purchased the columns, swans, pedestals and bowls to bring back to Kansas City.

The eight pink marble columns, each 12 feet high, with bases and capitals of white marble, form the backdrop for two fountains in the small Mission Hills park. Steps lead from the columns to an oval pool with a large pedestal of Carrara marble. Four swans on the main bowl support a smaller top bowl. The top bowl empties water into the larger bowl, which in turn falls into the oval pool below. Beyond the oval pool lies a 50-foot-long rectangular pool with small water jets. The park is south of the intersection of Mission Drive, Ensley Lane and Overhill Road.

By 1985 vandals and the harsh Kansas weather had taken a toll on the columns and the fountains. Mission Hills city council member Betty Lu Duncan noticed the damage and encouraged the city to fix the problem. In 1986 the council voted to spend $48,290 to repair the columns and fountains. Residents contributed more than half the money for the restoration; 16 residents donated more than $500 each.

In 1997 the Mission Hills council voted to pay for a structural inspection of the Verona Columns to make sure they wouldn't fall over. Earlier inspections confirmed that they had been leaning, Pisa-style.

In the 1920s J.C. Nichols and his employees often traveled abroad, buying small artworks and figures to dress up new Nichols housing developments. The statues on this page stand guard on streets that feed into Shawnee Mission Parkway.

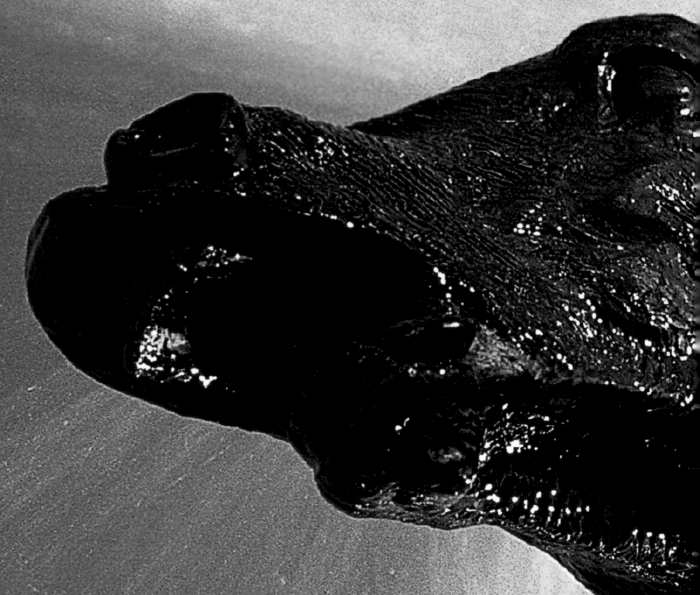

COUNTRY CLUB PLAZA
city of art

Detail of the J.C. Nichols Fountain on the Country Club Plaza.

The Kersting family remembers one of its own — daughter Megan — during a Kansas City Hospice memorial service at the J.C. Nichols Fountain.

▶

Prom dates Alissa Block and Jonathan Keys gaze into the fountain on a warm spring night.

CHAPTER 8: COUNTRY CLUB PLAZA
city of art

The J.C. Nichols Memorial Fountain is Kansas City's signature fountain. It is the city's favorite place for pitching woo or pitching for causes.

When it's warm, couples stroll around the fountain hand in hand, sit close by on benches and embrace as nine jets splash water on the statues in the background.

Politics, protests and memorial services draw Kansas Citians to the site year-round: to oppose a presidential appointment, to protest aid to a foreign government, to decry ballot-counting irregularities, or to hold a candlelight vigil.

Situated just north of 47th Street between Main Street and J.C. Nichols Parkway, the Nichols Fountain supplies the perfect backdrop for any event covered by the media. There's the quaint Moorish architecture of the Country Club Plaza and the lush greenery of Mill Creek Park. It's a bucolic setting for newspaper and television pictures. And the visibility is near perfect on this high-traffic corner – motorists at several intersections can see demonstrators clearly.

The Nichols Fountain evokes a sense of timelessness, even though it's only been here since 1960. During the 1950s the city, the parks board and business groups

together decided to honor J.C. Nichols by building the fountain and placing it adjacent to the Plaza, the shopping district that Nichols built to anchor his suburban housing developments in southwest Kansas City and northeast Johnson County.

In 1957 the parks board and the city agreed to construct a fountain with an 80-foot diameter. The city appointed a committee of businessmen to solicit donations and oversee construction. Designers placed the fountain in the center of an X-pattern of sidewalks that divide the south end of Mill Creek Park.

The parks and recreation department donated the land, moving a Daughters of the Confederacy monument to 55th and Ward Parkway to make way for the fountain. The city pledged some of the funds to build the fountain, though the majority came from businesses and individuals. The children of J.C.

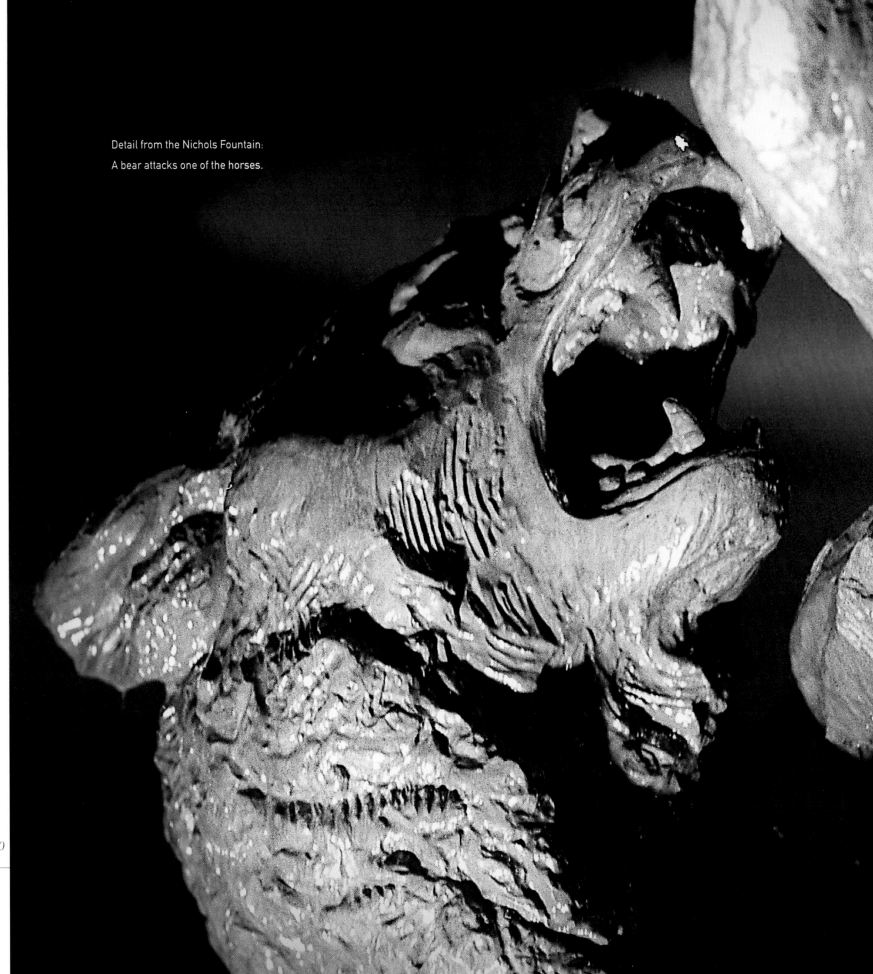

Detail from the Nichols Fountain:
A bear attacks one of the horses.

Nichols donated the statuary, which they'd acquired from an estate on Long Island, New York, in 1952, two years after Nichols' death.

By 1959 the central tier of the fountain and the basin were finished, and some water jets had been installed and had begun flowing. Parks workers installed the statuary just before the formal dedication of the fountain in 1960. The dominant statues are four horses, each with riders. Two riders appear to be battling animals, one an alligator, the other a bear. The horse figures sit within the basin at cardinal points. Between each sit smaller bronze figures of children and dolphins, each with water jets. The figures were sculpted in France and cast in bronze.

For years parks officials fought an ugly tan patina that covered the statuary. They frequently cleaned and polished the statues, only to have the film return after the water was turned back on. In 1998 officials finally found a way to prevent the film from coming back. They discovered that the rusting pipes that fed the fountain's sprayers were to blame for the discoloration of the statuary. When they installed stainless steel plumbing, the tan slime went away.

People aren't supposed to splash in Kansas City's fountains. Nevertheless, summer strollers are regularly seen pulling off their shoes and dipping their feet into the Nichols fountain; sometimes rowdy teen-agers take the plunge on a dare and jump in all the way.

From political demonstrations to popping the question, the J.C. Nichols Fountain seems to be the perfect place for expressions of passion.

162

J.C. NICHOLS FOUNTAIN (1960)

Art historians say the four equestrian figures in the
Nichols Fountain might represent four continents,
or four of the world's biggest rivers – or they could
symbolize man's struggle through life. The fountain
was built in 1959 and dedicated a year later.

THE GIRALDA TOWER (1967)

The Country Club Plaza features
Spanish colonial architecture, including
this half-size model of the Giralda
Tower in Seville. The landmark tower is
on the corner of J.C. Nichols Parkway
and 47th Street.

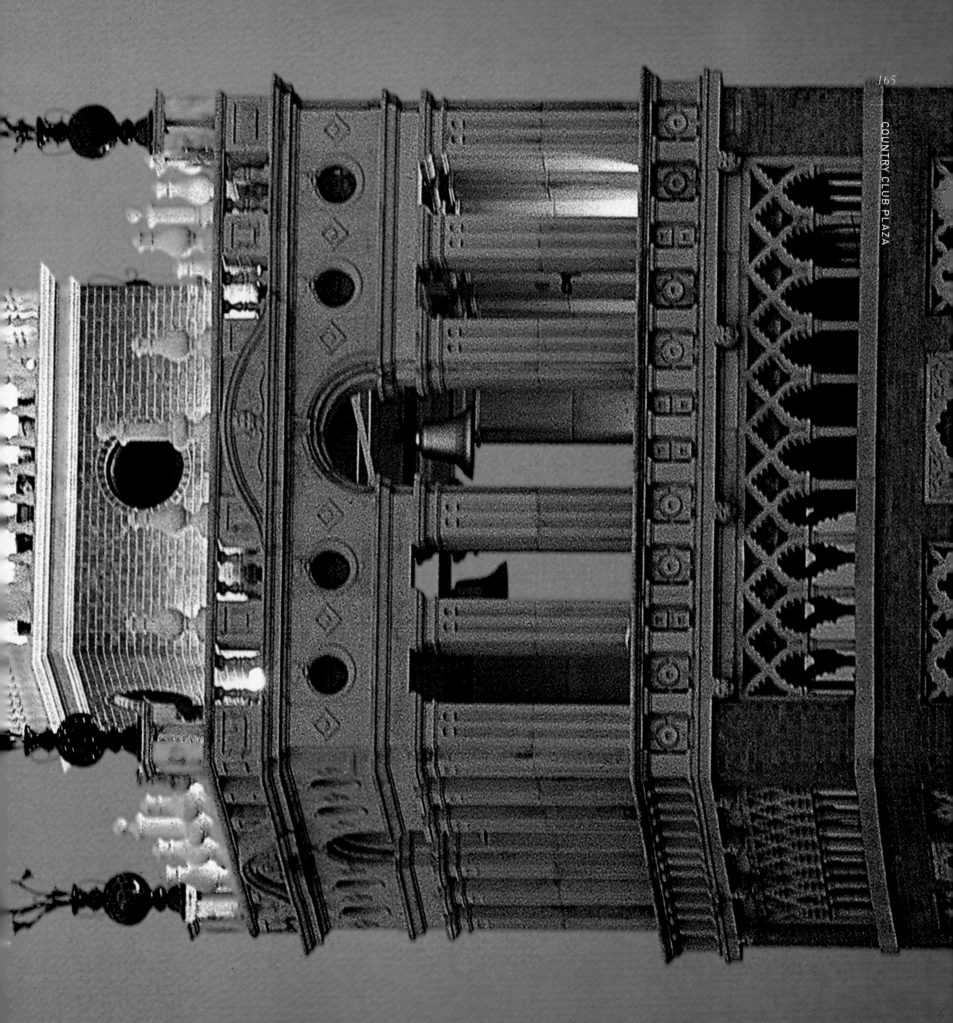

DIANE: SITTING (1976)

This Richard McDermott Miller sculpture is the centerpiece of the fountain at 4720 Jefferson St.

THE NEPTUNE FOUNTAIN (1953)

Miller Nichols, son of J.C. Nichols, found the Neptune
Fountain in the warehouse of a Kansas City scrap-metal
dealer. The 8,000-pound cast-lead fountain sits in an
oval pool at 47th Street and Wornall Road. The three
seahorses are said to move Neptune's chariot through
the water.

This bench, across from the Fairmont Hotel, is adjacent to the "Married Love" sculpture.

SLEEPING CHILD (1995)

The original marble figure by Andreini of Florence, Italy, reclines on a traffic island at 47th Street and Broadway.

FOUR FAUNS (1958)

The "Four Fauns" squirt water into a rectangular pool on Nichols Road just east of Broadway. Only one is an original; the other three are castings made to replace fauns that were stolen.

THE PAN FOUNTAIN (1969)

This fountain had to have special footings made to support the 10,000-pound sculpture. In this detail, a female figure with wheat sprigs in her hair holds a cornucopia as she touches a child figure.

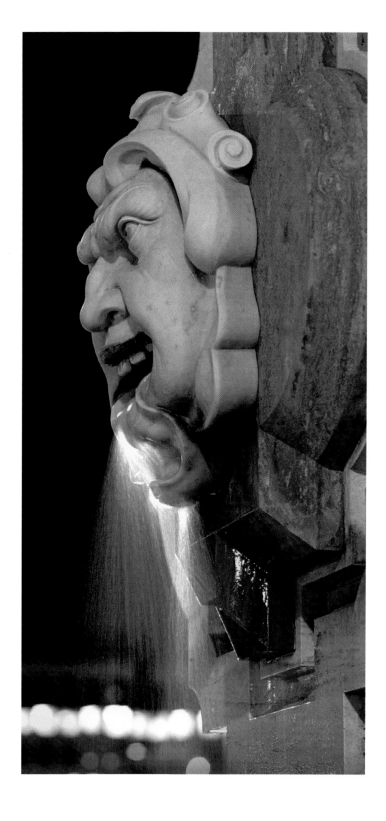

THE SEVILLE LIGHT FOUNTAIN (1967)

This is a replica of the fountain in the Plaza de los Reyes
in Seville. Spain. It sits on a traffic island on J.C. Nichols
Parkway at 47th Street.

This bust of a lion is one of many architectural adornments brightening buildings on the Plaza.

When J.C. Nichols began planning the Country Club Plaza, he and his architects decided to use Spanish design motifs: stucco, ornamental ironwork, and tile for roofs, walls and artwork. Nichols envisioned the Plaza not only as a shopping center but also as the gateway to his residential developments to the south in Kansas City and to the west across the state line in Kansas.

CANCER...
    THERE'S HOPE (1990)

The Richard and Annette Bloch
Cancer Survivors Park, dedicated in
1990, supports people with cancer,
survivors of cancer and their families.
This sculpture is by Victor Salmones.

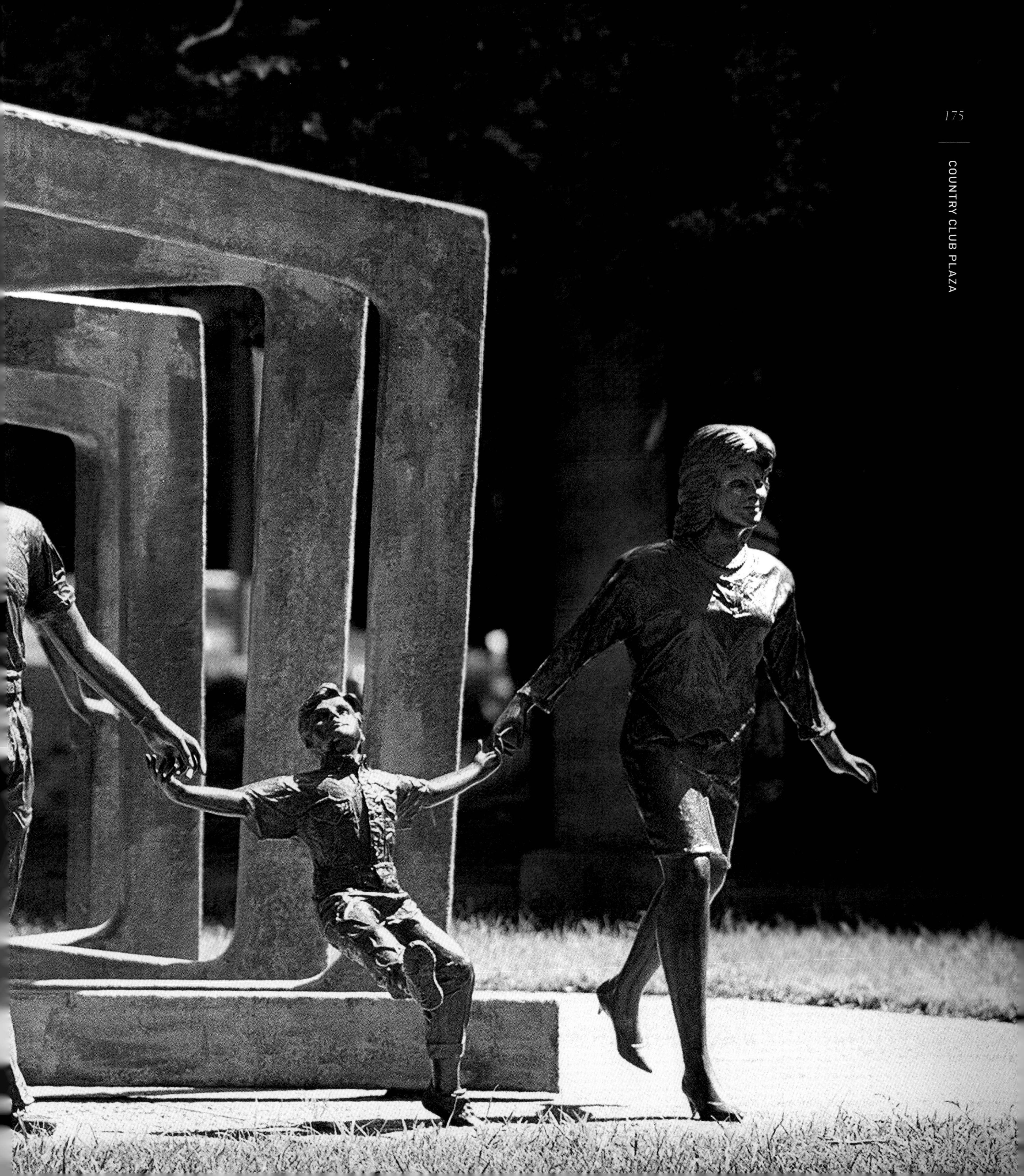

◄

▲

MERMAID
FOUNTAIN (1930)

The child is the centerpiece of
this Plaza fountain that features
mermaids.

MARRIED LOVE (1984)

This piece by Oscar Nemon depicts British Prime Minister Winston Churchill and his wife,
Clementine, seated on a bench, with Clementine looking toward her husband. The statue was
created for its location at the southwest corner of the bridge at Wornall Road and Ward
Parkway. Nemon, who knew Churchill for 30 years, had created a much smaller version of the
statue for Blenheim Palace, where Churchill was born and married.

MASSASOIT (1979)

Cyrus E. Dallin, creator of "The Scout" in
Penn Valley Park, also sculpted this piece.
It stands west of Winstead's on 47th Street
on the Plaza. Massasoit, a Wampanoag
Indian, befriended the Pilgrims who settled
in Massachusetts. Mr. and Mrs. Miller
Nichols paid for the statue, which was
moved from its original location on the
west side of Main Street to accommodate a
street expansion.

AFTERWORD
city of art

In the past 10 years Kansas City's public art landscape has become vibrant. Consider just a few of the works that have appeared: Bartle Hall's "Sky Stations," the spiders at the Kemper Museum, and "Corps of Discovery," the Lewis and Clark statue in Case Park.

At the Nelson-Atkins Museum, the lawn has become a sculpture park, home to world-class Henry Moore sculptures and the whimsical "Shuttlecocks."

In addition to new sculpture, dramatic new public fountains have been built, the latest being the Bloch Fountain between Union Station and Liberty Memorial.

But for every new piece of art that's gone on display or fountain that's begun spraying, some work from the past has been neglected. The prime example is Liberty Memorial, before it was finally closed and then rescued by the taxpayers.

In particular, many of Kansas City's fountains have fallen into disrepair. During 2001, the year that material was gathered for this book, the Volker and Vietnam Veterans fountains were late to be turned on because repairs weren't done. Volker, at the south end of Theis Park between the Nelson-Atkins Museum and Midwest Research Institute, was being rewired, even though taxpayers had paid $1.2 million to move, renovate and improve it in 1996. The Vets fountain waited for

weeks for a new pump. The fountain at Barney Allis Plaza and the Sea Horses at City Hall were late sprayers, too.

In Blue Valley Park at 23rd and Topping, the Heritage Fountain, an 85-foot tower with 16 nozzles on top, stands dry. Water has undermined the terraced deck – in fact, this one hasn't produced a squirt in years. And it's not scheduled to be fixed. The parks department says it would take as much as $500,000 to repair it.

There are other fountains that haven't sprayed in years, too: in Swope Park, on the Paseo, across from the Concourse. And there are those that spray but look shabby.

The real travesty, however, is the Swope Memorial, a colonnade, a plaza, a fountain and a scenic overlook in Swope Park. The parks department constructed the memorial in three stages from 1917 to 1931 to honor Thomas Swope, the man who gave Kansas City the land for Swope Park, one of the largest urban parks in the country.

Broken steps now lead down to the memorial, which was built into a hillside, on the northwest side of the Swope Memorial Golf Course. The colonnade frames a marble terrace that holds Swope's crypt. Two flights of marble steps, some of them broken, too, drop to a plaza with a bowl fountain that should cascade water into a reflecting pool. But this fountain holds only rainwater. To the west, the Kansas City Zoo

and Starlight Theatre peek out from the opposite hill.

If the Swope Memorial were repaired and the brush cut back, the view would be stunning, the setting tranquil. As it stands, it's decrepit – more like a relic of ancient Rome. Some of the responsibility for these lapses belongs to Kansas City's Parks and Recreation Department; other organizations are sometimes responsible, too. Parks officials complain that they don't have adequate funds to keep every statue clean, every memorial maintained and every Kansas City fountain running. But that's what the citizens of Kansas City ought to expect.

It should be a matter of pride. You see, we Kansas Citians aren't the only ones enjoying these public artworks. When we claim to be "one of the few livable cities left," or the "city of fountains," then we should prove it to the tourists and business travelers who visit us. You'd never see St. Louis neglect the Gateway Arch, or San Francisco disregard the Golden Gate Bridge.

Kansas City is more than barbecue and the home of late, great musicians. We get a sense of place from our public art and our fountains. Let's make sure our statues are protected and our fountains pumping. They are an integral part of our identity. They reflect who we are.

– *Tim Janicke*

LISTINGS AND MAPS
city of art

LISTINGS *and maps* (artworks listed in order of appearance in book)

1. WALKING MAN
   (ON THE EDGE)
   *Quivira Road and College
   Boulevard*

2. SKY STATIONS
   *Bartle Hall, Truman Road
   and Broadway*

3. THREE WAY PIECE
   NO.1: POINTS
   Nelson-Atkins Museum

4. THREE FIGURES,
   FIFTEEN ELEMENTS
   *Kansas City International
   Airport entrance road*

5. SPIDER
   Kemper Museum

6. BULL WALL
   American Royal Arena

7. BULL MOUNTAIN
   Interstate 670 and Genessee

8. LIGHT STEEPLE
   *Community Christian Church,
   4601 Main*

9. ISLAND GARDEN
   *Highway 50, 10 miles east
   of Lone Jack*

10. TRIPLE CROWN
    2600 Grand Boulevard

11. HENRY WOLLMAN
    BLOCH FOUNTAIN
    Pershing Road, west of Main

12. PIONEER MOTHER
    Penn Valley Park

13. CORPS OF DISCOVERY
    Case Park, Eighth and Jefferson

14. MUSE OF THE MISSOURI
    *Main Street between Eighth
    and Ninth*

15. THE SCOUT
    *Penn Valley Park, east of
    Southwest Trafficway*

16. JAMES PENDERGAST
    MEMORIAL
    Case Park, Eighth and Jefferson

17. BIRD LIVES
    17th Terrace and Vine

18. PIONEERS
    Broadway and Westport Road

19. LUG
    *City Hall, 12th Street
    between Oak and Locust*

20. MONUMENT, POLICE
    HEADQUARTERS
    12th Street and Locust

21. CATHEDRAL OF THE
    IMMACULATE CONCEPTION
    411 West 10th Street

22. SUNDIAL
    9th Street and Broadway

23. ABRAHAM LINCOLN AND TAD
    *City Hall, 12th Street between
    Oak and Locust*

24. HARVESTER
    *Courtyard northeast of 11th
    and Walnut*

25. RAIN THICKET
    *Oppenstein Memorial Park,
    12th and Walnut*

26. MUSE OF THE MISSOURI
    *Main Street between Eighth
    and Ninth*

27. POWER & LIGHT BUILDING
    14th and Baltimore

28. A BRUSH OF TIME
    3217 Troost Avenue

29. MURALS
    *West end of Avenida Cesar
    E. Chavez*

30. MODERN COMMUNICATION
    *Emergency Communications
    Center, Locust, between 11th
    and 12th Street*

31. TEAM ILLUSION
    *87th Street Parkway and
    Lackman*

32. TWO ON BEAM
    *JCCC, Quivira Road and
    College Boulevard*

33. BETWEEN THOUGHT
    AND FEELING
    *JCCC, Quivira Road and
    College Boulevard*

34. FLIGHT OF IMAGINATION
    *JCCC, Quivira Road and
    College Boulevard*

35. HARE AND BELL
    *JCCC, Quivira Road and
    College Boulevard*

36. PERFORMANCE PIECE
    *JCCC, Quivira Road and
    College Boulevard*

37. WOMAN WITH PACKAGES
    *JCCC, Quivira Road and
    College Boulevard*

38. CHILDREN OF THE
    TRAILS MEMORIAL
    Johnson County Courthouse

39. GROWING
    Leawood City Hall

40. JOY OF LIFE
    *Rockhill Road and Volker
    Boulevard*

41. CITIZEN SOLDIER
    *Veterans of Foreign Wars
    headquarters, 34th and
    Broadway*

42. GEORGE WASHINGTON
    MEMORIAL
    *Grand Boulevard and Pershing
    Road*

43. SHIVA
    *Grand Boulevard and Pershing
    Road*

44. STONE LIONS
    *Kansas City Life Insurance
    Company, Broadway and
    Armour Boulevard*

Note: Item 26 reads RODINRODANNADANNA / *Ninth and Central*

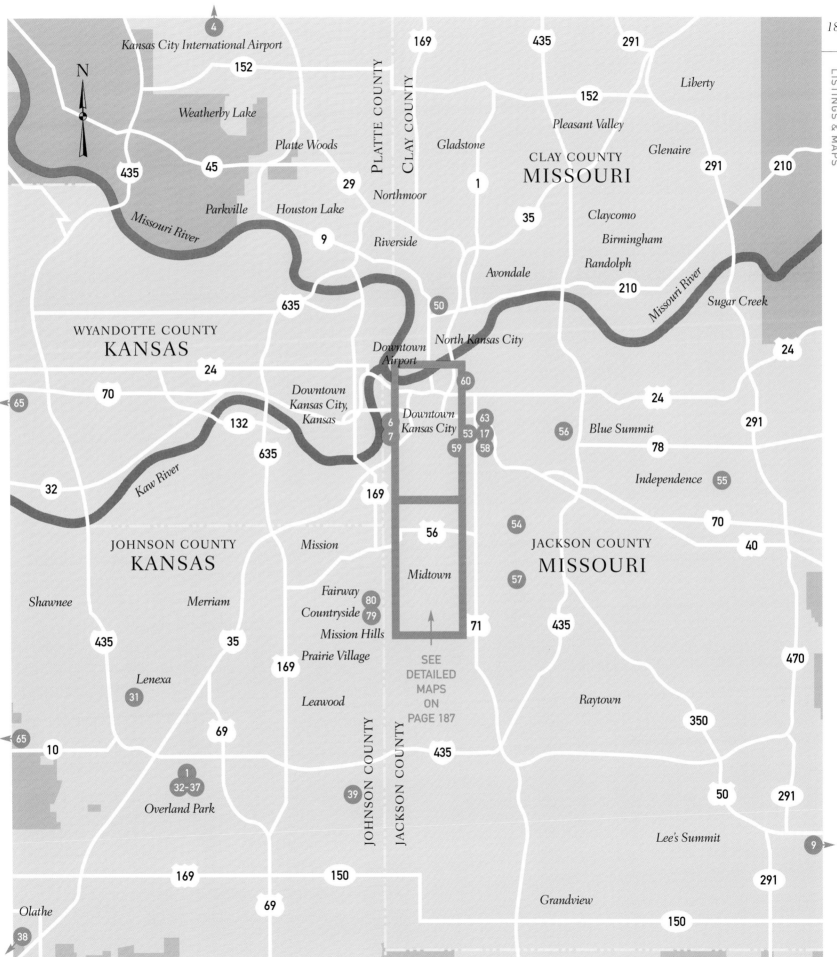

4

Kansas City International Airport

152

N

169   435   291

Liberty

Weatherby Lake

152

Pleasant Valley

Platte Woods

Gladstone

Glenaire

CLAY COUNTY
MISSOURI

435

45

PLATTE COUNTY

CLAY COUNTY

291   210

1

291

29

Northmoor

Claycomo

Parkville

Houston Lake

35

Birmingham

Missouri River

9

Riverside

Randolph

Avondale

210

Missouri River

Sugar Creek

635

50

WYANDOTTE COUNTY
KANSAS

North Kansas City

Downtown
Airport

24

24

24

70

Downtown
Kansas City,
Kansas

60

291

65

Downtown
Kansas City

63

56   Blue Summit

132

6   53   17

78

635

7   59   58

Kaw River

169

Independence   55

32

JOHNSON COUNTY
KANSAS

Mission

56

54

Midtown

70

JACKSON COUNTY
MISSOURI

40

57

Shawnee   Merriam

Fairway   80

71   435

Countryside   79

435   35

Mission Hills

470

Prairie Village

169

SEE
DETAILED
MAPS
ON
PAGE 187

Lenexa

31

Leawood

Raytown

350

69

JOHNSON COUNTY

JACKSON COUNTY

65

50   291

10

435

1

32-37

39

Overland Park

Lee's Summit

9

169   150

Grandview

69

291

Olathe

150

38

45 LIKE PETALS UNFOLDING
45th and Main

46 HOPE FOR LIFE
*Rockhill Road and Volker
Boulevard*

47 VOLKER FOUNTAIN
*Oak Street and Volker
Boulevard*

48 LOOSE PARK WALL
FOUNTAIN AND JACOB
LOOSE STATUE
*Loose Park, 51st and
Wornall Road*

49 LIBERTY MEMORIAL
Penn Valley Park

50 CHILDREN'S FOUNTAIN
*North Oak Trafficway and
Missouri Highway 9*

51 KAUFFMAN MEMORIAL
GARDENS
4800 Rockhill Road

52 FIREFIGHTERS MEMORIAL
FOUNTAIN
31st and Penn Valley Park

53 SALVATORE GRISAFE
MEMORIAL
The Paseo and 16th Street

54 SPIRIT OF FREEDOM
*Cleveland and Brush Creek
Boulevard*

55 COMMUNITY OF CHRIST
TEMPLE
*River Road and Walnut,
Independence*

56 UNTITLED, FIRE STATION
6600 Truman Road

57 THE RACE IS NOT ALWAYS
TO THE SWIFT!
*Lakeside Nature Center,
Swope Park*

58 SPHINX
*Scottish Rite Temple, Linwood
Boulevard and The Paseo*

59 URBAN PALISADE
1200 East Linwood Boulevard

60 CONCOURSE
St. John Avenue and Gladstone

61 THE EAGLE
Ward Parkway at 67th Street

62 AVENUE OF THE TREES
*Ward Parkway, south of Meyer
Circle*

63 LAMP POSTS
*Bruce R. Watkins Drive at
the Paseo*

64 COLUMNS
*Ward Parkway at Gregory
Boulevard*

65 MOSES
*Smith Hall, University of
Kansas*

66 SHUTTLECOCKS
Nelson-Atkins Museum

67 SEATED WOMAN
Nelson-Atkins Museum

68 LARGE INTERIOR FORM
Nelson-Atkins Museum

69 SHEEP PIECE
Nelson-Atkins Museum

70 STANDING FIGURES
(THIRTY FIGURES)
*Nelson-Atkins Museum
(removed during construction)*

71 THE THINKER
*Nelson-Atkins Museum
(removed during construction)*

72 THREE BOWLS
Nelson-Atkins Museum

73 STORAGE
*Nelson-Atkins Museum
(removed during construction)*

74 RUSH HOUR
*Nelson-Atkins Museum
(removed during construction)*

75 EAST GATE PIECE
Kansas City Art Institute

76 THOMAS HART BENTON
STATUE
Kansas City Art Institute

77 SEVEN VIEWS OF THE
GRAND CANYON
Kemper Museum

78 MEYER CIRCLE FOUNTAIN
*Ward Parkway at Meyer
Boulevard*

79 BELINDER COURT FOUNTAIN
Tomahawk and Belinder

80 VERONA COLUMNS
*Mission Drive, Ensley Lane
and Overhill Road*

81 J.C. NICHOLS FOUNTAIN
*47th Street between J.C.
Nichols Parkway and Main*

82 GIRALDA TOWER
*J.C. Nichols Parkway and 47th
Street*

83 DIANE: SITTING
4720 Jefferson

84 NEPTUNE FOUNTAIN
47th Street and Wornall Road

85 SLEEPING CHILD
47th Street and Broadway

86 BENCHES
*Wornall Road and Ward
Parkway*

87 FOUR FAUNS
Nichols Road and Broadway

88 PAN FOUNTAIN
Jefferson and 48th Street

89 SEVILLE LIGHT FOUNTAIN
*J.C. Nichols Parkway and
47th Street*

90 CANCER...THERE'S HOPE
*Southwest Trafficway and 47th
Street*

91 MERMAID FOUNTAIN
Nichols Road and Broadway

92 MARRIED LOVE
*Wornall Road and Ward
Parkway*

93 MASSASOIT
47th and Main Streets

Maps by John Sopinski

There are many people to thank for help in creating this book.

Heidi Iverson Bilardo, the interim administrator of Kansas City's Municipal Art Commission, guided me with lists of art pieces and with the knowledge of what was considered significant by the experts. Terry Rynard, assistant superintendent of Kansas City's Parks and Recreation Department, patiently returned my calls, explaining which fountains were being repaired, which weren't and how to find them. The City of Fountains Foundation supplied an elaborate map of Kansas City fountains. And the scholarly book published by the foundation in 1985 was a gold mine of historical information.

Kansas City Star reporters Matt Campbell and Tim Engle contributed stories, as did *Star* art critic Alice Thorson. Tim also edited the copy and proofed the pages, sometimes into the early hours of the morning. *The Star*'s library helped me find historical information.

Several *Star* photographers offered their work. John Sleezer's opening photograph of the Bartle Hall "Sky Stations," David Pulliam's pictures of the Power & Light Building and Keith Myers' "Bull Mountain" stand out.

Thanks go to my boss, Mary Lou Nolan, head of *The Star*'s features department, who let me produce this book around my regular *Star Magazine* duties; to Star Books publisher Doug Weaver, who was willing to postpone this project until trees were leafing and spigots spraying so that I could get good pictures; to this book's designer, Jeff Dodge, who understands that "God is in the details" and that "less is more." And to Doug Worgul, my editor and former boss, who supplied inspiration during desperation.

Thanks go to my children, Andrew and Natasha, who waited patiently for me to come home, and who may now finally believe that I really was photographing and writing a book.

And to my wife, Paula, who for the past seven months has been both mommy and daddy: I love you. I'll be home – tonight!

– *Tim Janicke*